Gary,

SELF-LOATHING
FOR BEGINNERS

Merry Christmas - 2009

Tim · Nancy

SANTA
MONICA
PRESS

SELF-LOATHING FOR BEGINNERS

HELLO
my name is

~~Fleur~~
Deeply Flawed

LYNN PHILLIPS

Published by: Santa Monica Press LLC
P.O. Box 1076
Santa Monica, CA 90406-1076
1-800-784-9553
www.santamonicapress.com
books@santamonicapress.com

S A N T A
M O N I C A
P R E S S

Printed in the United States

Santa Monica Press books are available at special quantity discounts when
purchased in bulk by corporations, organizations, or groups. Please call
our Special Sales department at 1-800-784-9553.

ISBN-13 978-1-59580-029-9
ISBN-10 1-59580-029-8

Library of Congress Cataloging-in-Publication Data

Phillips, Lynn, 1945–
Self-loathing for beginners / by Lynn Phillips.
p. cm.
ISBN 978-1-59580-029-9
1. Conduct of life—Humor. 2. Self-help techniques—Humor. I. Title.

PN6231.C6142P45 2008
818'.609—dc22
2007041437

Cover and interior design and production by cooldogdesign
Worm illustrations by Lynda Jakovich/cooldogdesign

Cover image: © Photographer: Didier Kobi I Agency: Dreamstime.com

CONTENTS

Introduction

" . . . thou canst not think worse of me than I do of myself."

—*The Anatomy of Melancholy* (1621), Robert Burton

BEING YOUR own worst critic, as Robert Burton realized, is something to boast about, because no one else knows enough about you to loathe you as well as you can. Bragging rights aside, if you have ever experienced as much as a twinge of self-loathing, you probably didn't want to call attention to it; you may even have loathed yourself a little for feeling it.

But properly done, the desire to jump out of your skin into something more comfortable can goad you on to great acts of self-improvement, make you much more compelling to both lovers and paparazzi, and bring you far more success than you feel you deserve.

The trick is to do it right. That means putting your self-loathing to work for you, so that whether you are trying to hide it or flaunt it, escape the pain of it, or to see how much of it you can stomach, you use your self-loathing to make life more interesting.

Luckily, new avenues for self-loathers abound: DIY porn, warts-and-all high-definition TV, obesity epidemics, not to mention government-sanctioned torture and omigod-we've-killed-our-ecosphere chic—none of these high-potential fields were open to self-loathers a decade ago. And you can still access the classic paths to self-loathing, like mistaking your hostess for her mother or drinking your marriage into oblivion.

Yet most beginners quickly discover that successful self-loathing isn't as easy as it looks. Extracting a masterpiece of self-contempt from one's social gaffe or inability to stay sober (or faithful) is an art; and, as with any art, raw talent isn't enough: you must study your craft and its traditions if you expect to have your squirming self-doubt taken seriously. Yet no one (until now) has offered the novice any formal instruction in the basics of self-loathing, let alone the techniques of the masters.

Self-Loathing for Beginners aims to meet that need. Drawing upon numerous disciplines—from neuroscience to the E! Channel—it will help you style your self-loathing so that you can lend poignancy to the inevitable trials of life and make your lighter side (if you have one) pop, even against a boring pastel background.

Should you hope to rid yourself of self-loathing or turn it from a leopard into a lap dog, this book is not for you. But if you agree that anything worth doing is worth doing with awareness and enthusiasm, I can help you to develop your self-loathing potential more economically and painlessly than any of the competing methods, including periodontal work. So if you miss the vogue for loving your self-loathing, you'll have no one to blame but yourself.

—Lynn Phillips, New York, NY

PART I
THE BASICS

"WHAT IS MAN MADE
OF, THAT HE MAY
REPROACH HIMSELF?"

—WERTHER, IN "THE
SORROWS OF YOUNG
WERTHER" (1774),
JOHANN WOLFGANG
VON GOETHE

CHAPTER 1

The FAQ

"I have had just about all I can take of myself."

—S. N. Behrman (1893–1973)

THE GREATEST misconception beginners have about self-loathing is that you have to be loathsome to excel at it. Not true. The greatest charm of self-loathing is that once you get the hang of it, you can detest yourself regardless of your actual worth. Luckily, self-loathing, besides being as arbitrary in its distribution as love, is a lot easier to create out of thin air.

Acts of true evil? These are optional, although I rarely recommend them. Hating yourself for hacking the heads off Hutus is, face it, a bit too obvious. And besides, do-gooders often self-loathe better than villains.

Denzel Washington feels worse about himself for each African child he can't save than Saddam Hussein ever felt about using chemical weapons on the Kurds.

Once beginners realize that self-loathing does not oblige them to do anything as horrible as ethnic cleansing, they are usually overeager to jump right in and start rejecting something about themselves they can put their hands on—like their bodies. But before exploring the verdant fields of bodily self-loathing, I recommend savoring these next two short chapters on the basics before moving on to more entertaining matters, like toe jam, nose hairs and celebrity jowls.

ARE YOU A BEGINNER?

Note to Readers: Throughout *Self-Loathing for Beginners* (*SL4B*), I answer questions commonly asked in workshops and online discussion groups, and also questions you might be embarrassed to ask but which I decided to go ahead and put into your mouth anyway. As "your" queries are repeatedly rewarded with useful answers, you will begin to appreciate how displaying your humiliating ignorance can speed up the learning process. (This lesson alone is the equivalent of an Ivy League education.)

YOUR QUESTIONS ANSWERED

Q: What's a beginning self-loather?

A: A beginning self-loather is someone who has stopped believing flatterers, suck-ups, brown-nosers, toadies, sycophants, boosters, Pollyannas and infatuated groupies, but is not too sure what to do next.

Q: Will I need any special equipment?

A: The most important piece of equipment you can bring to this endeavor is you. As you work to cultivate your self-loathing, try not to rest on your tiny beginner's laurels (or should I say "laurel"?). Your job is to always strive, strive, strive, strive, strive for things beyond your grasp. Beyond that, feel free to use whatever motivational totems you like—a flail, a worm costume, or a voodoo doll of yourself full of pins might help. Snapshots in which you have extra chins or madness in your eye can give your self-loathing a boost. Jeans that no longer fit may also inspire you.

Q: Do I have "the right stuff" to be a self-loather, or am I spinelessly self-forgiving?

A: Like a talent for tying knots or shopping while drunk, self-loathing aptitudes vary. Near zero, you'll find the late actress-turned-filmmaker, Leni Riefenstahl, whose agitprop documentary, *Triumph of the Will,* made Hitler's fascist revolution look as hot as a Calvin Klein ad. Critics begged her to denounce her Nazi past, but she was so self-loathing-impaired that she died at age 101 without ever uttering those two little words, "My bad." Among the self-loathing-challenged you will also find Paris Hilton (see Impairment Box, page 62) and Vanity Smurf.

Near the opposite extreme are changelings. Changelings abhor themselves so totally, so intensely, that to survive their own scorn they must turn into someone or something else.

Most changelings turn into eerie replicas of whatever type of person ridiculed them in high school. Young Andrew Warhola, snubbed as an effeminate, blotchy-faced nobody by the in-crowd, erased his vulnerable high school self and replaced it with "Andy Warhol, pop artist," the emotionally vacant ruler of an underground glamour empire.

A host of ugly duckling actresses who later became swans, like Liv Tyler ("I had braces, permed hair, and was chubby"), appear to be changelings, but they retain their inner dorks, and work with their early self-loathing rather

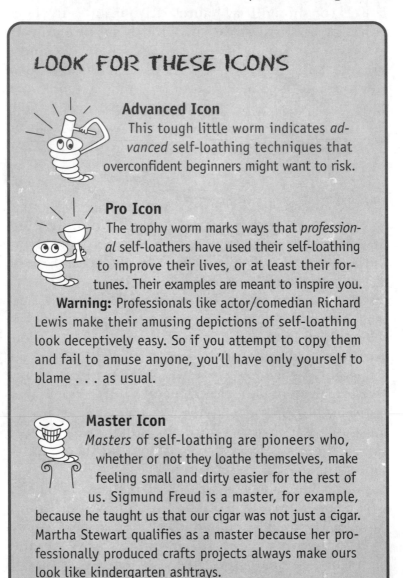

LOOK FOR THESE ICONS

Advanced Icon
This tough little worm indicates *advanced* self-loathing techniques that overconfident beginners might want to risk.

Pro Icon
The trophy worm marks ways that *professional* self-loathers have used their self-loathing to improve their lives, or at least their fortunes. Their examples are meant to inspire you.
Warning: Professionals like actor/comedian Richard Lewis make their amusing depictions of self-loathing look deceptively easy. So if you attempt to copy them and fail to amuse anyone, you'll have only yourself to blame . . . as usual.

Master Icon
Masters of self-loathing are pioneers who, whether or not they loathe themselves, make feeling small and dirty easier for the rest of us. Sigmund Freud is a master, for example, because he taught us that our cigar was not just a cigar. Martha Stewart qualifies as a master because her professionally produced crafts projects always make ours look like kindergarten ashtrays.

than amputating it. Most of us, like Tyler, fall between the extremes of the self-loathing-impaired and changelings. Our mix of private doubts and public humiliations help us wriggle our way down the waterslide of self-debasement— as the television program *American Idol* has shown.

DO YOU HAVE WHAT IT TAKES TO SELF-LOATHE?

Take this quick test to find your place on the self-loathing aptitude scale. Check off the statements that best represent your secret thoughts or feelings of self-doubt or self-rejection, and see your results below.

I don't know if I loathe myself exactly; I just can't stand . . .

- ☐ My voice on tape
- ☐ My love handles (saddlebags, muffin-top, man-breasts, hairdo, hairy mole, missing nose)
- ☐ My habit of interrupting people before I know what they're talking about (what I'm talking about, how important they are)
- ☐ My failure to come up with anything interesting or amusing to say (do, buy)
- ☐ My obsessive self-preoccupation
- ☐ The number of times I've been just plain wrong about Iraq
- ☐ My taste in men (women, sycophants, casual flings, accountants)
- ☐ The way I pig out when stressed
- ☐ The way I pig out when my only excuse is, "Somebody else bought the donuts"

☐ That I can't afford _____ (a Picasso, a jet, a co-op, a vacation, dinner)

☐ That I envy _____ (Cameron Diaz, Tiger Woods, Tweezerman)

☐ My readiness to sell out

☐ My readiness to sell out way too cheaply

☐ My dependence upon _____ (psychoactive substances, high-risk sex, apologies)

☐ How much time I waste on stupid quizzes

☐ How greatly I resemble those I hold in contempt

☐ My morning breath

☐ My entire life

Now count your check marks and evaluate your results:
1 check mark = Leni Riefenstahl
18 check marks = Andrew Warhola

HOW MUCH SELF-LOATHING IS ENOUGH?

Q: Do I have to loathe all of myself, or can I start with smaller bits?

A: You would think that utter self-loathing would be the brand of choice for every ambitious contender, but utter self-loathers tend to burn out too quickly to do anything very interesting with their gift—beyond hanging themselves from rafters. And, although the few who succeed, like grunge rocker Kurt Cobain, earn Master status by inspiring millions of others to cringe at the very thought of themselves, many believe that Cobain's widow, partial self-loather Courtney Love (see Inspiration Box, page 171), will rack up more hours of quality self-loathing before she dies.

So the average beginner will do best to stick to partial self-loathing. In fact, most professionals achieve acclaim and all that goes with it by choosing only one sliver of themselves to loathe, and then making a huge production out of it.

Remember: It really doesn't matter to anyone how much of yourself you loathe as long as you do it in a fascinating and shameless manner.

Part-time self-loathing of every kind—episodic, sporadic, Saturday night or Sunday morning self-loathing—is easier to fit into a busy schedule. As a beginner, start by waking up with a vague malaise. Direct it towards self. Review past failures, especially failure to visualize self as happy, successful, and impervious to the bitter envy of less fortunate people; that is, people like you. To amp up your feelings of inadequacy, exploit insomnia and rain (when available) or else bad dreams in which a giant foot is descending upon you.

Flaw Flaunters

Cindy Crawford marketed the scary mole on her lip as a "beauty mark," and used her most visible flaw to stand out from the supermodel pack. Jon "Napoleon Dynamite" Heder manages something similar in comedy with mouth-breathing.

By evening, after a punishing day in an unfeeling world washed down with a glass of overpriced swill, you will be ready to start again in the A.M.

Warning: Don't try combining morning and evening self-loathing if you want the benefits of part-timing.

SELF-LOVE— FRIEND OR FOE?

Q: I'm sorry to say I sometimes love myself. Will that interfere with my self-loathing?

A: Good news here, too: partial self-loathing mixes well with approving, even worshipful feelings about yourself. In fact, self-love and self-loathing go together like strawberries and cream, or piss and vinegar.

You can love yourself one day and hate yourself the next, or love yourself from the neck up while hating yourself from the knees down. You can love yourself for

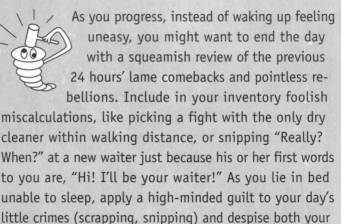

As you progress, instead of waking up feeling uneasy, you might want to end the day with a squeamish review of the previous 24 hours' lame comebacks and pointless rebellions. Include in your inventory foolish miscalculations, like picking a fight with the only dry cleaner within walking distance, or snipping "Really? When?" at a new waiter just because his or her first words to you are, "Hi! I'll be your waiter!" As you lie in bed unable to sleep, apply a high-minded guilt to your day's little crimes (scrapping, snipping) and despise both your petty cruelties *and* your inability to enjoy them with wicked glee.

Professional self-loathers can apply part-time self-loathing techniques to the future by alternating bursts of self-fulfilling pessimism ("I'll never learn to self-loathe better than Kirstie Alley!") with healing stretches of cock-eyed optimism ("I can too loathe myself better than Kirstie Alley! I know I can!").

BONUS
SELF-ESTEEM
QUOTE

"Self-esteem: the worst sickness known to man or woman, because it says, 'I did well, therefore I am good,' which means that when I do badly—back to shithood for me!"
—*Albert Ellis on his 90th birthday celebration at the Albert Ellis Institute, 2003*

being among the few who still read books, but hate yourself for reading books of advice like this one by someone who doesn't even know you.

Many self-loathers get anxious when they feel self-love because they are afraid that the relationship will get out of hand and destroy the self-loathing that makes them special, but this is a needless fear. The more you love yourself, the easier it is to put up with your self-loathing, to show it off, and—once you've learned to show it off with confidence—to enjoy the attention self-loathing gets you.

COMBINING PARTIAL SELF-LOATHING WITH PART-TIME SELF-LOVE

1. The Oil-Spill Method

An oil-slicker's self-love and self-hatred don't mix, and when they meet, it's a mediagenic event. The call-in radio host and anti-liberal Rush Limbaugh is the classic example. On air, he exuded self-love while ranting against drug addicts. In private, he was hooked on OxyContin. When his addiction was revealed it was a widely enjoyed scandal. Note that oil-spillers like Limbaugh, unlike hypocrites, aren't pretending to be what they are not. They really *are* their own "evil twin." (See also The Haggard Method, page 157.)

2. *The Cocktail*

Like a Cosmopolitan or Manhattan, the cocktail blends an intoxicating dose of self-loathing with the sweetness of self-admiration and does it so well that the mélange goes down more smoothly than either ingredient alone. Simply put, professional cocktail types find their own loathsomeness adorable. One of the most notable of this expanding category is actor James Spader, whose message is, "I know I'm pasty-faced and kinky. That's why you want me." (See Larry David Inspiration Box, this page, for more cocktail-style self-love-and-loathing.)

3. *The Parfait*

The most inspiring specimen of the self-love and self-disgust parfait is philanthropist and yo-yo dieter Oprah Winfrey. Oprah is able to layer her public self-love and private self-loathing like low-fat whipped cream and sugar-free Jell-O so that both can be tasted distinctly, but at the same time. Whereas someone like Janet Jackson merely replaced her younger self with a re-engineered entertainment product, the point of Oprah's "you-go-girl!" makeover is to remind everyone (including her) of how bad she felt about herself before it, and, somewhere under the diet Cool Whip, always will. It's the ferocity of her ever-present adversary that makes

Curbed

Cocktail mixologist Larry David, the star and creator of *Curb Your Enthusiasm*, celebrates (among his many other failings) his inability to feel apologetic about the things he loathes himself for. In fact, the more he self-loathes, the more pleased with himself he is.

her battle to love herself exciting rather than saccharine.

4. *The Time-Release*

Time-Releasers are those who express their disgust with themselves more and more as they age, until people have little else to marvel at. Watching the evolution of the seductive Young Elvis into the terrifyingly demented Old Elvis was like sneaking into Dorian Gray's attic and watching his portrait develop. Overall, there is no greater audience-pleaser than a time-release exhibit of professional self-loathing, as Sly Stallone has discovered. (See also Donatella Inspiration Box, page 204.)

 **Tip**

If you want to build a great self-image without sacrificing self-loathing, you can make a great parfait by giving your baby a distinctively awful name, like "Moonbeam," "Lourdes," or "Scooter." That way you can feel clever and creative but at the same time loathe yourself for dooming your child to decades of taunts.

5. *The Side Dish*

Perhaps the most respected way that professionals display their mixed feelings about themselves is side dishing. It's also the easiest for beginners to learn. When your self-loathing starts crushing your self-love rather than complementing it, you restore your self-admiration by undertaking good works, like buying a purse from a struggling Sri Lankan co-operative or installing a thermal cooling system in your summer mansion. The success of this trick depends not on the amount of actual good you do, but on convincing yourself (and others) that the kind, magnanimous person is the main course, and the bruised and self-rejecting egomaniac is only a side of broccoli rabe.

PERPETUAL MOTION SELF-LOATHING

QUESTIONS FROM THE FLOOR

Woman with scary eyebrows and red nails: If my career goal is to become a professional self-loather, which of my character traits should I loathe most?

SL4B: You can loathe any or all of your character traits once you get into the rhythm of it. "I'm too bloody nice for my own good" is just as useful as "Why am I such a raving bitch?"

A Little on the Side

Princess Diana was the queen of all side-dishers. Both her husband's devotion to an older woman and the snobbish scorn of the royals caused her such shame she was having trouble keeping her dinner down. She began to identify with children living in old war zones who, like her, were being mangled whenever hidden remnants of past hostilities suddenly exploded in their faces. To distract the English (and herself) from her growing disgust with herself at having mistaken a minefield of a relationship for a fairy-tale marriage, Di generously campaigned to defuse the thousands of land mines buried in poor areas around the world. For that, she still holds the side-dish crown, even though Madonna and Angelina have both put in their orders for the title.

THE PING-PONG PADDLE ICON . . .

. . . indicates opportunities to loathe yourself this way or that: "pock, pock . . . pock, pock . . ." Your objective in this game is to keep over-shooting the thin net of perfection and land in the zone marked "flawed."

If you can't loathe yourself for being too reticent, you can loathe yourself for being too yappy.

or

If you judge your character harshly, you're self-punishing. If you don't, you're deluded.

THE FREE PASS

Cynical dude in old T-shirt: If I judge myself harshly, do I get a free pass to judge other people harshly too?

SL4B: Ah. The "free pass." The tortured self-loather's favorite rationale: "In despising others I am only being even-handed." You will be as sorry as I was to learn that if you are a self-loather who is being as hard on others as you are on yourself, you're just being cruel. This sort of cruelty, however, is a wonderful entry-level character flaw to loathe yourself for.

ONE LAST QUESTION

Q: Do dogs and cats self-loathe?

A: Some, yes. But fish, like clams and chipmunks, have different issues.

Master of Comprehensive Self-Loathing: Robert Burton (1577–1640)

The Anatomy of Melancholy, quoted at the beginning of SL4B's Introduction, is Burton's over-1,000-page compendium of everything a 17th-century scholar could know about feeling lousy—from bilious humors to piles. While most of the science in it is outdated, the book still accurately—and wittily—portrays self-loathing as a difficult companion we must learn to live with rather than a noisy drunk who can be thrown out on his ear.

THIS CHAPTER'S MANTRA

I must learn from
the mistakes of others
because I am not smart
enough to create any
on my own.

CHAPTER 2

The Building Blocks of Self-Loathing

"IS THAT *ME*?! MY GOD! IT *IS*!!"

—*Self-Loathing Comics*, '94–5,
Robert Crumb

LIKE ANY field of endeavor, self-loathing has rules and core principles. A beginner will want to master these, if only to misapply them later.

Here are . . .

SELF-LOATHING'S SEVEN ESSENTIAL QUESTIONS (AND THEIR ANSWERS)

Essential Question #1: Will I need a self to loathe?

A: Absolutely! As a general rule, extremists who have shed their egos may be self-abnegating, even self-destructive, but they are no longer self-loathing. The selfless include certain martyrs, terrorists, saints, mystics, and rulers when they are engulfed by role and ritual. Mother Teresa, despite her religious devotion, had a self to loathe; Mohammed Atta, unfortunately, did not.

Essential Question #2: Do I need a coherent belief system in order to despise myself, or will any random opinion work?

A: Your pick. You can identify with someone you think has a consistent set of values, like Jesus or Posh Spice, then loathe yourself whenever you fail to live up to your ideal. But you'll also do fine by grabbing at various values on the fly. That way, every fashion spread, every self-help article, every fundraising mailer will suggest to you new and refreshing ways to hang your head in shame.

Another excellent method is to develop your own sacred credo, a personal set of commandments you don't even know you have, and which are impossible to obey. Here are the most popular . . .

TOP 10 SECRET COMMANDMENTS FOR SELF-LOATHERS

1. THOU SHALT NOT COMPROMISE THY PRINCIPLES, EVER.

2. THOU SHALT BE BEST AT EVERYTHING, ELSE THOU HAST FAILED.

3. THOU SHALT BE CHILL; LET NOTHING GET TO THEE.

4. THOU SHALT ESCHEW BANALITY, NOR BE ORDINARY.

5. PLEASE THEE THY CRAZY PARENTS, BE THEY SATIABLE OR BE THEY NOT.

6. THOU SHALT FEED THE HUNGRY— EVERY LIVING ONE OF THEM.

7. FEEL AT ALL TIMES HAPPY, FOR MOODINESS IS AN ABOMINATION.

8. REMEMBER: TO ERR IS REGRETTABLE, TO FORGIVE THYSELF, DEFEAT.

9. THOU SHALT TRUST THY OWN JUDG- MENT, YEA, EVEN WHEN THOU ART NUTS.

10. THOU SHALT NOT SELF-LOATHE.

These, of course, are not written in stone, and if you discover that you have come up with others, please append them or make substitutions on your own initiative. Just be sure that they are flawless in phrasing and insight.

The values you choose—whether selected for integrity, variety, or futility—don't matter. The main thing is to have some standards that you take seriously enough to make self-disgust or self-condemnation inevitable.

Essential Question #3: Must I do something that violates my beliefs, opinions, values, or standards?

A. Exactly! If you think being a short, hairy little Greek is repulsive, you must be short, hairy, little, and Greek. If you think that seducing your best friend's lover (or lover's best friend) makes you despicable, you must do exactly that. Intellectual? Try mispronouncing "synecdoche" at a book party. In construction? Drop your hammer from five floors up onto a stack of new windows. Ardent opponent of racism? Develop an erotic fixation on white women or black men. Violate away!

The point? You can't self-loathe if you never disappoint or appall yourself.

 **Tip** Having trouble finding beliefs, opinions, or values to violate? Try believing "Thou shalt have values," then loathe yourself for lacking any!

 Advanced self-loathers cover the waterfront with the caveat: "Be perfect."

 Once you get to be a professional, you can castigate yourself for not being tops in the self-loathing field.

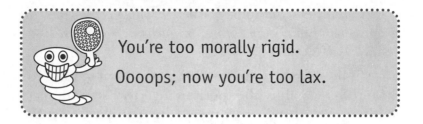

You're too morally rigid.
Oooops; now you're too lax.

Essential Question #4: What if I don't believe it's my job to judge myself?

A: Some people believe that only God is fit to judge them. Others believe that their mother's forgiveness nullifies their guilt, or even that we are all expressions of divine will and therefore blameless. Such believers cannot properly self-loathe. But those who hang onto any of these convictions after being downsized, savaged by the press, sued for divorce, and covered with painful boils by the God they thought loved them are very, very rare. (See story of Job, page 183.)

Many beginners judge themselves harshly even though they believe that they have no right to judge themselves at all. Recognizing your own hypocrisy in these instances only makes you feel more interesting. (See page 30 on violating one's own standards and convictions.)

Essential Question #5: Will shining a positive light on everything I am or do prevent me from self-loathing, the way it seems to do for oil industry lobbyist and U.S. vice president Dick ("Things are going well") Cheney?

A. Not inevitably, I'm happy to say. And seeing through your own spin well enough to self-loathe has a lot of mass appeal. (See Inspiration Box, page 33.)

Essential Question #6: If I'm incapable of experiencing disgust, revulsion, shame, rage, or queasiness can I still successfully self-loathe?

A: The short answer? Yes and no. To self-loathe, you have to be capable of experiencing vivid sensations of loathing. But this doesn't mean that you have to suffer them at the exact moment of self-detestation. Self-loathers who dread the gut-churning of self-rejection often repress their gag reflex and continue to self-loathe without being aware of it until they do something self-punishing or deadly, like becoming a host on *The View* or eating a box of Krispy Kreme doughnuts. The point is, if these "Who, ME?" self-loathers never felt revolted by themselves, they wouldn't be so desperate to imagine that they currently don't.

Essential Question #7: Is it possible to have all six of the factors you just listed working for me, and still be unable to organize them all into a complete self-loathing kit?

A: Sadly, yes. You can have (1) a clear sense of self, (2) a belief system (however transient) that (3) you are willing to violate, (4) a self-critical streak, (5) a talent for seeing though your best self-deceptions, and (6) an ability to feel disgusted—but still not know how to (7) bring all these assets together into one vibrant

 **Tip**

A great boomer trick is to:

1. Achieve beatific detachment using whatever: drugs, alcohol, and flirtations with people considerably younger or older than you. Then, at the very moment of transcendent self-acceptance, the moment in which you feel serene and beatific . . .

2. . . . look in the mirror at that insanely grinning face full of swarming pores and blotches.

3. Realize that the face is yours.

4. Experience the Tao of psychedelic disgust faster than you can say "Like, wow. I'm a gnome."

spasm of self-loathing. But luckily, assembling self-loathing from its components is a skill that can be drummed into most of us, and, hopefully, the remainder of this book will do just that.

FOUR SIGNS THAT SELF-LOATHING IS IN THE HOUSE

Most of us don't have time to review each bout of self-loathing to make sure that all elements are present. Here are a few quick ways to tell:

Pundit Possessed!

Talking head Bill O'Reilly is the king of punctured self-deception. A champion of "traditional values" who has been busted for initiating phone sex with age-inappropriate subordinates, O'Reilly clearly knows that he's not who he tells himself he is. Even while he is projecting righteous confidence on his talk show, *The O'Reilly Factor*, you can see the swarm of self-tormenting demons fly out of his ears to chomp on his buttocks before zooming around his waist to rub his tummy with a loofah. It's no surprise that U.S. TV viewers can't get enough of this man!

1. You have just gotten something you've been dying to get (the Nike account, spanked by a stranger in an alley, both, etc.). Instead of rejoicing, however, you want to puke.

2. You're thinking, "If only I had torn myself away from CSI long enough to study, that would be me up there receiving my Ph.D. in _____ (molecular physics, Serbian epic, plant psychology)."

3. Somebody at the table says they've never experienced a single minute of self-loath-

ing, and that somebody isn't you, and you wish you weren't you either.

4. It's Monday.

WHAT TYPE OF "WHO, ME?" SELF-LOATHER ARE YOU?

Denial-prone self-loathing comes in many different styles. See if you can find yours among the two most popular:

1. Catapulters—in a frantic effort to ignore their self-loathing, catapulters pack their self-hatred into Molotov cocktails and lob them at others. Favorite targets include Jews, Muslims, gays, women, Mexicans, imperialists, poor people, and bigots. Evangelist and pundit Pat Buchanan is a genius at this, his inner pain giving a bright glow to his anger. Rosie O'Donnell's running battle with Donald Trump has a catapult edge. Even if it's only a publicity stunt, it's hard to otherwise explain how she could feel so much passion towards a man with such bad hair.

2. Oscar Winners—are so busy competing for various prizes they have no time to notice how much they loathe themselves, but at moments of victory they all suddenly break down and cry.

Now, see if you can match these "Who, ME?" self-loathers to their style. Circle the categories that best match:

C = CATAPULTERS   O = OSCAR WINNERS

1. Roy Cohn—C or O (See Roy Cohn Inspiration Box, page 158)
2. Sally Fields—C or O (See Abject Insecurity Quote Box, page 68)
3. Jennifer Hudson (*American Idol* ex-finalist and Effie White in the film *Dreamgirls*)—C or O
4. Mel Gibson—C or O (See "Does He or Doesn't He?" page 196)

Answers: ᴐ 'ㄣ 'O 'ɛ 'O 'ᄅ 'ᴐ 'ı

ONE LAST QUESTION

Q: Can I possibly accomplish all that self-loathing requires while sober?

A: Not if you haven't had a drink or missed an AA meeting in two years.

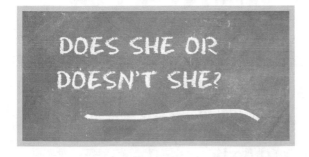

Madonna

Madonna was able to summon up the first six ingredients of self-loathing and then get prudes to do all the loathing for her. By systematically shocking the pants off anyone who might possibly disapprove of her for any reason (slut, sacrilege, kinks, materialism, etc.), she turned her every spasm of self-loathing into a mischievous and profitable game instead of anything she had to actually experience. The one occasion for self-loathing she hasn't shopped out to others is middle age. (See Inspiration Box, page 187.) Verdict: She didn't, but now she does.

Master of Basic Self-Loathing: Nicolaus Copernicus (1473–1543)

By proving that the earth revolves around the sun rather than the other way around, Copernicus unseated humanity from the front row in God's VIP skybox and stuck us in the bleachers of the solar system where the floor is sticky and the view obstructed by beefy fans. Thanks to him, it became vastly easier for everyone to feel ignored, marginal, and insignificant. For this, we revere him.

THIS CHAPTER'S MANTRA

It isn't whether
I win or lose,
it's how badly
I do both.

CHAPTER 3

Self-Loathing's No-Brainer— The Body

" . . . the body rots, sags, stinks, is covered with warts and pores and bumps and blemishes of all sorts; and one experiences what little beauty the body does have, and what little excitement it is able to produce, less frequently and less intensely the more one comes in contact with it."

—*The Plague of Fantasies* (1997), Slavoj Žižek

YOUR BODY is the easiest part of yourself to loathe, because unlike your mind, it can't argue with you about how vile it is. Additionally, it goes through appalling stages, so that just as you get used to its being skinny and awkward, it becomes tumescent and hairy (and less attractive than someone else's), then it gets polluted, then wrinkled and flabby, then most of it gets converted into silicone or prosthetics until it isn't even yours anymore. If you complain about it, your body just sits there like a pathetic sponge mop, soaking up your abuse. And no matter how you pamper it, your body will wither and die, taking you with it. Think about it in the right way and you'll realize: there is nothing to love about your body—and that's a great start.

This chapter assigns self-loathing exercises to men and women separately, but feel free to replace your body parts with those of the other sex and find them as hilariously wrong as the originals. In any case, there's no need to be gender-appropriate here.

Bodily self-loathing can be fun and exciting. It can inspire you to get rich creating products and services for other bodily self-loathers to buy, use, and become disillusioned with. It's supposed to send you running to the gym or the diet aisle or the bed of someone whose beauty makes you feel like a lump of suet. Here you will learn to savor your self-loathing at its most up-close and personal.

WOMEN FIRST

Whether a Heidi Klum or a Dame Edith, an attentive self-loather will find her body an endless source of material. A recent survey published in *Grazia* magazine revealed that 98% of women hate their bodies, and concluded that the average British woman worries about her body every 15 minutes, which is to say 66 times a day if she's getting her beauty rest and 74 times a day when she's up all night worrying about who really wrote *Macbeth*.

Match the Celeb to Her Bodily Self-Loathing

Celebrity Body	What she loathes about it:
a) Heidi Klum—swimsuit supermodel, *Project Runway* host, actress	1. "I have cellulite"
	2. Doesn't like to show her "bum, thighs, and legs."
b) Tara Reid—*American Pie* actress (before correcting botched plastic surgery)	3. Says she has "a bottle opener" of an overbite.
	4. Used to often feel "unattractive."
c) Jessica Alba—actress	
d) Keira Knightley—*Atonement* actress (accused by press of anorexia)	5. Says she has "cellulite" plus "a big booty" and a forehead that makes her look like a "Light-Bulb Head." Also "dark circles under my eyes," and "No matter how much I work out, I never get muscle tone in my butt and hip area."
e) Tyra Banks—supermodel	
f) Angelina Jolie—actress, philanthropist, child-adopter	
g) Eva Mendes—actress and Revlon spokesmodel	6. "I'd love to have tits but I don't—I have pecs."
h) Jessica Biel, *Esquire*'s "2005 Sexiest Woman Alive"	7. Wishes she was both "less curvy" and thinner.
i) Salma Hayek—*Frida Kahlo* actress and producer	8. Self-described "Frankentummy." Said her areolas look like "goose eggs."
j) Donatella Versace, fashion designer and mogul	9. "I hate my legs"
k) Felicity Huffman—Lynette Scavo on *Desperate Housewives*	10. "I had that 'Just can't be thin enough' thing. 'Hate my body, hate my body, hate my body.' You sort of top off at throwing up about six times a day because your body just can't take it anymore."
l) Jessica Rabbit—buxom cartoon star of *Who Framed Roger Rabbit?*	
	11. "I hate to see myself."
	12. "There's nothing I hate about my body."

Answers:

a) 9; b) c) 8; d) 7; e) 5;
f) 4; g) 3; h) 2; i) 1;
j) 11; k) 10; l) 12

YOUR QUESTIONS ANSWERED

Women loathe so many things about their bodies and its parts that we're going to take questions about the easiest—called "The Six Favorites"—first. Then we'll insert a subsection on men's bodily self-loathing, returning to women's most intense body issues—known as "The Four Ghastlies"—once the men have rolled over and gone to sleep.

Favorite #1: Size

Q: What's the best approach to hating my size?

A: Oh, come on! You know this one. Simply decide that you, or parts of you, are too large or too small. Breasts, buttocks, hips, belly, nose, and thighs are particularly prized by women given to partial self-loathing.

When you are too hurried or lazy to itemize sections of your body to loathe, loathing your overall weight is a great time-saver. Hating your weight also triggers disgust with yourself for devouring the foods you crave (see Part II, Chapter 6), so that eating them yields a double helping of self-loathing in the time it takes to prepare just one.

Additionally, studies show "fat talk" is an effective bonding ritual you can perform with women of every subculture, class, or marital status, including Diana Ross, Roseanne Barr, Renée Zellweger, and Calista Flockhart to name just a few. Simply bring up the topic of weight, vocalize your self-loathing, and you'll get all the excitement of intense female competition without the tears. An "I'm too horribly fat" contest is one of the few you can win without exciting envy.

The trick with hating your overall size, and, in fact, the secret behind many self-loathing success stories, is to be droll about the loathsomeness potential of your height or width before meaner people have time to draw a bead on it. "Built for comfort, not for speed" is an over-used but otherwise handy template, because it advertises not only your discomfort with your excess flesh, but also your ability to handle the discomfort without a lot of help. Try "Built for comfort, not for compliments," if you are unhappy with your width, or, "I was going to wear stilettos, but I wanted to be able to tell you from an ant," if you are over 5'11". If you're skinny, go heavy on the schtick, with lines like, "Yes, you think I'm skinny now; but when I was six, my mother used to mistake me for a piece of fettuccine. I'd wake up with Alfredo sauce all over me. And the dog would have to lick it off before I could go to school." Self-deprecatory humor should be delivered deadpan, or with a faint smile, the objective being to declare your vulnerability without seeming to wallow in it. If none of these techniques work for you, do what most women do and pretend to be interested in others.

Favorite #2: Shape

Q: Are there any special tricks I need to know if I want to hate my shape?

A: Yes. Now that J. Lo has made big booty fashionable, bemoaning your "fat ass" may not work you up to the pitch of revulsion you're after, and you'll have to concentrate on your rear end's more subtle demerits like its lack of loft or the sine of its curves. Since hating the shape of your ass now demands something close to a degree in engineering, you might want to make your job easier by (1) disparaging the shape of another body part or area while (2) using competitive comparisons. For example, "Hers looks like melons, but mine look like goat testicles," or, "Your upper arms may look like sticks, but mine look like drumsticks."

In this liberal age, you are now permitted to envy boys as well, provided you do it with maximum gender bending, as in: "My husband looks better in my bustier than I do," and "I'd give up sex with women if I could have Brad Pitt's hips."

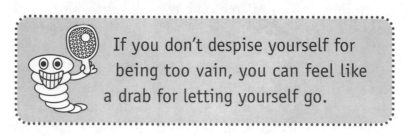

If you don't despise yourself for being too vain, you can feel like a drab for letting yourself go.

Favorite #3: Proportions

Q: What if I love all my various parts, but still want to loathe my body?

A: Let science come to your rescue. Numerous studies show that people are most strongly attracted to physical symmetry, so find asymmetry in any of your matched parts and you're good to go.

Is one of your breasts inconveniently perfect? No worries, as long as the other one isn't. The asymmetry suggests to the mate-seeking part of observers' animal brains that something isn't quite right with you. It's an opinion that, despite your better judgment, the feedback-dependent self-loather in you will instantly adopt.

And what if the kinky John (*"Hairspray"*) Waters or sophisticated Diana Vreeland areas of your brain prefer the poignancy of flawed-beauty-verging-on-the-grotesque? No worries again. Those sections of your brain can easily despise both the beer-swilling frat boy of your animal brain—with its yearning for symmetrical, matchy-matchy "prettiness"—and the feedback-dependent part of you that actually cares what beer-swilling frat boys think.

The proportion of your body parts can repulse you in other ways. Use your words. Tell yourself, for example: "My head looks like a grapefruit perched on a redwood tree stump," or, "If I was a foot and a half taller, my tits would make me look like Pamela Anderson instead of the fucking *Venus of Willendorf*!" If you're coming up empty, improvise something along the lines of, "I look like somebody finally tried to splice Julia Robert's head onto a Chihuahua."

Favorite #4: Hair

Q: If my hair is sleek and falls well, is there any hope for me?

A: Try to arrange a bad haircut, an overcooked dye job, or disastrous perm—all easily and inexpensively obtained at nearly any neighborhood salon. Otherwise, a dip in a chlorine pool followed by a lazy day in the sun should do the trick.

Meanwhile, here are 25 things to loathe your hair for *not* being:

1. Straight

2. Curly

3. Silky

4. Shiny

5. Longer

6. Shorter

7. Blonder

8. Whiter

9. Darker

10. A richer red

11. Full of "natural highlights"

12. Full of "vibrant" color

13. Clean

14. Tousled

15. Sleek

16. Thicker

17. Finer

18. Wavy

19. Soft

20. Fuller

21. Well-cut

22. Easy to style and maintain

23. More plentiful on your head than under your arms or on your upper lip

24. Somebody else's

25. Real.

Favorite #5: Face

Q: Which is more self-loathing, wearing a burqa to hide my face or getting a complete facial transplant?

A: That depends on whose face you sew on. But women who want to avoid acquiring a face-donor's flaws along with her strong points are ordering new facial features à la carte, using *People* magazine as their catalogue. In 2007, according to The Beverly Hills Institute of Aesthetic and Reconstructive Surgery, the most requested items included: Scarlett Johansson's lips; Sienna Miller's eyes; Jessica Alba's nose; Ziyi Zhang's cheeks; and Oprah Winfrey's charge card.

Favorite #6: Skin

Q: What is the most important thing to hate my skin for not being?

A: Three years old.

With women's "Six Favorites" under your belt, let's take a brief intermission and let men hate their bodies for a while before tackling the most emotionally swampy portions of the female.

MEN CAN DO IT TOO

THE SEVEN MANLY QUESTIONS

Manly Question #1

Q: Am I doomed to feel left out of the physical self-loathing festival?

A: Not at all. As a man, your physical self-loathing can run silent but deep. Cut to the chase and begin by giving your penis one or more of these juvenile and belittling names . . .

Name It . . .

Either . . .	Or . . .
	Customize, filling in the blanks.
Mr. Pencil	Moby the ____
Mr. Softee	____ the Perform-
(Mr. Anything)	ing Worm
Weenie	Hank the ____
The Hoff (see *Impairment Box*, page 48)	____ the Milk-Spitting Snake
My pet goat	Cleopatra's ____
Freckles	____ the Pocket Rocket
Tiny Tim	Porky, Corky ___y
Fitty cen'	_____ Potter
A penis called "It"	Tricky _____
	____ the Dangler

Manly Question #2

Q: What if I totally love my penis, no matter what I call it?

A: Compare it to others, using this army-issue checklist:

Combat-Tested Penis Comparison Checklist

_____ My penis is too small (shorter, or thinner than you believe normal—or both).

_____ My penis is too small compared to my father's (stepfather's, mother's boyfriends').

_____ My penis is too small compared to the high school quarterback's (basketball center's, head of chess club's, drill sergeant's, garbage man's).

_____ My penis is way too small compared to penises of other races (religions, ethnic groups) or general expectations concerning my own race (religion, ethnic group).

_____ My penis is too small compared to the size of my ego.

_____ My penis is too soft.

_____ My penis ejaculates too quickly, or so my (ex-) lovers all claim.

Manly Question #3

Q: Oh, insecurity about the penis. Everybody does that. Can't I hate my hanging gut? And what about the bagels in back of my neck, and my hip-cheeks?

A: Traditionally, if you want to be "one of the guys," those things are best left to others to loathe. To stay comfortably in the majority, loathe your receding hairline and bald spot. (According to *The Economist*, roughly the same number of American men are having their hair "revived" as women are having their breasts "augmented.") Many men choose to advertise how much they loathe balding by combing wisps of hair over the bare skin atop their heads, by having weird little tufts of hair surgically implanted in the thinning area, or by running for office.

Tip Self-loathing on a budget? Two mirrors, angled so that you can follow the progress of your male pattern baldness is all you really need. That and a bottle of shoe polish.

POP QUIZ

A. Name two famous comb-overs.

B. Name two famously bad toupees.

C. Name two pre-emptive head shavers.

Answers:

A: Zero Mostel & Barney Frank (or Rudy Giuliani)

B: Howard Cosell & Ted Koppel (or Sam Donaldson)

C: Bruce Willis & Yul Brynner (or Sinéad O'Connor)

Manly Question #4

Q: What if I would rather hate my muffin-top and these sort of breast thingies than be "one of the guys"?

A: I lied. It's increasingly manly to fuss and fret about being flabby, blubbery, having a pumpkin butt, all that. The American Society of Plastic Surgeons reported a

10% increase in male liposuction requests between 2004 and 2005, mostly to reduce the "spare tire." (As we all know by now, over half of all adult Americans are either overweight or obese.) Men have even begun seeking calf implants, and, according to Popbitch, the U.K. gossip e-rag, the testicle lift is "the in-demand plastic surgery for rich, aging Hollywood men." So start saving up.

Manly Question #5

Q: *How about the hair on my back, my sack, and my crack?*

A: If you wax your body hair and you sleep with women, you can loathe yourself for being a metrosexual.

Impairment Box

Annals of the Self-Loathing Impaired

Actor David "The Hoff" Hasselhoff's 16-year-old daughter, Taylor, made him a YouTube star by releasing a video showing him lying half-naked and out-of-shape on the living-room rug—dumb drunk, and trying, between slurred mumbles, to eat a disintegrating hamburger with his hands while she cajoled him to sober up. He later attributed his alcoholic "relapse" to "a painful divorce," and thanked his daughter for making the tape to "show me what I was like," so he could get "back on my game." But it was a self-loathing-impaired apology. Why? Because a true self-loather would have mentioned that in Taylor's video he looked more interesting as a ruin than he ever did in all his studly antics on *Baywatch*.

Or, if you're a gay guy who waxes and tries to pass for a metrosexual, you can loathe yourself for being in the closet. Otherwise, wait until the stubble grows in, and hate that. But in most circles, back, sack, and crack hair still fall into the "for others to loathe" category. Still, you can take heart: the masculine knack for uncritical self-acceptance is on its last leg. Male body-anguish is on the rise. And even if you can't keep up with the times, when you get older, regardless of your sexual orientation, you'll be able to loathe the hairs that grow out of your ears and nose—especially if you use them to form a comb-over.

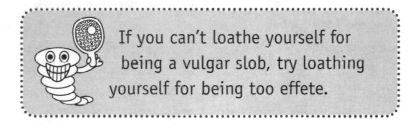

If you can't loathe yourself for being a vulgar slob, try loathing yourself for being too effete.

Manly Question #6

Q: If I'm great looking now, does that mean that I am going to end up looking like a surprised prune when I'm old, the way Robert Redford, Kenny Rogers and Burt Reynolds do?

A: Only if you can afford all that work.

Manly Question #7

Q: Can't I hate my body's secretions, my vomit, excrement, zits, moles, buboes, boogers, warts, farts, suppurating ulcers, dandruff, toe jam, sweat, blood blisters, skin tags, and scabs without considering them parts of my body?

A: What are you, some kind of girl? No way. Even metrosexuals know that the body's exudations are part of the deal, however transient they may seem. True, your body is more than its pus and earwax, piss, seed, and night soil, but if you work hard and pay attention, you can forget that.

To boyish men who love all their disgusting physical extrusions and emissions because they enjoy the power of making women say "Eeeew!" . . . two words: "Marry me."

One Last Manly Question

Q: May I loathe the millions of bacteria that live in my gut without which I would die?

A: Because they are separate, if symbiotic life forms, loathing them does not really count as self-loathing. But, since you owe them your life, hating them is a form of ingratitude, and you might want to loathe yourself for that.

Master of Male Bodily Self-Loathing: Polykleitos of Sikyon

A physical ideal based on some "objective" or measurable standard dates back at least to 450–440 BC when the sculptor Polykleitos created the *Doryphoros*. This marble mannequin was designed to show a man's ideal proportions, using mathematical ratios. Base of nose to bottom of chin? One third of the face. Chin to hairline? One tenth of the whole body. Hand from wrist to middle fingertip? Same. You get the idea. (So did Leonardo da Vinci. See Inspiration Box, page 165.) The point was, Polykleitos came up with the notion of a perfectly proportioned man—and it wasn't him. Or you.

MEN'S BONUS MANTRA

"This has never happened to me before."

MORE WOMEN

THE FOUR GHASTLIES

Every self-loathing woman has her favorites in the ghastly category, which is known to Biblical literalists as, "What was God thinking?" and to atheists as, "If this is evolution, 'God help us!'"

FEMALE SELF-LOATHERS BEWARE

We're coming up on some material that may temporarily impair your ability to self-loathe with jaunty insouciance. If at any point this section revolts you, go and make a stab at "bodily self-acceptance" or "a realistic body image." Then, return when you have lost interest in upbeat self-delusions.

Ghastly #1: The Bust (More of Your Questions Answered)

Q: Do I have to be in show business to loathe my breasts?

A: No longer. In olden days, the only women who had their breasts stuffed were strippers like 1960s pioneer of topless dancing, Carol Doda. But *The New York Times* reports that the practice has spread to teens, cops, and women who live on credit. In 2006, according to the American Society of Plastic Surgeons, 329,000 enlargement surgeries were performed in the U.S. alone.

Q: How can I talk myself into this increasingly common badge of physical self-loathing?

A: Examine your breasts with the eye of a callow, 23-year-old porn addict. (Empathizing with someone even more repelled by your natural body than you are lets you hate yourself in their terms AND makes you hate yourself for identifying with them. It's a great technique to learn.)

Advanced self-loathers who want to loathe their breasts, may take inspiration from professional self-mutilator, the aforementioned Pamela Anderson: (1) Have bad implants; (2) follow with over-corrective surgical procedure; (3) return to plastic surgeon repeatedly, and (4) never get it right.

Ghastly #2: The Scent of a Woman

Q: Why do I so horrify myself when I hate the way I smell?

A: Science again: Smells bypass the rational frontal lobes and are processed directly in the emotional sewer lobe of the brain where our most carnivorous, humanoid, underground self-loathing dwells.

So, at certain times of the month, when you squat to pick up a fallen pencil or sock and catch a whiff of monthliness, allow the words "slaughterhouse" or "battlefield" to float up into your mind. If you want to get fancy, use the word "abattoir" and pronounce it with a French accent: ah-baht-TWAHHHR, and if you want to really be mean to your smell, try "rendering truck." The point is, when describing how foul you smell, don't be afraid of exaggerating. Doing so can pique your self-disgust and amuse everyone else. Declaring with sudden surprise, "Omigod! I reek of fecundity!" and making a horrified face will allow others to identify with you and recall with affection all the times they stank of vomit or Jack Daniels or both.

When your body isn't producing an odious stench on its own, try an overdose of Elizabeth Taylor's fragrance, Passions, as a substitute, particularly in elevators, theaters, and on the cross-country Greyhound bus. Then, whenever you see some cranky matron breathing through her mouth to avoid your aroma, use the reverse angle technique: (1) Feel her pain (2) Hate yourself for caring.

Ghastly #3: "Dimpling"

Q: Do I even have to ask?

A: No. Roughly 80% of women past puberty have cellulite, and close to 100% of them hate it. If you want to compete with them, learn to play with your cellulite in ways that are fun, but that in no way reduce your self-revulsion. Here are three suggestions to get you started:

1. Apply hideous or gross descriptions to your lumps: Wikipedia says that cellulite is "caused by the protrusion of subcutaneous fat into the dermis, creating *an undulating dermal-subcutaneous-fat junction with adipose tissue . . .*" See how medical terminology can disgust you even better than euphemisms like "hail damage," "sack of marbles," "the mattress phenomenon," and "cottage cheese?" If you can't remember to tell yourself that your buttocks suffer from a dermal-subcutaneous etc., try: "I look like I've been attacked by flesh-eating bacteria." Bingo!

2. Mirrors. Those in most dressing rooms, combined with the harsh lighting that sadistic merchandisers favor, will instantly turn the gentle rise of your thigh into a pitted dirt road trampled by wild hogs.

3. Hands on! Dig into your midriff. Turn it into an accordion of rubbery folds. Reach back and bunch

Tip

Tip for advanced self-loathers:

If you ever want to amp up your self-repugnance, and there are no cranky mouth-breathing matrons handy, imagine how revolted other people must be by your odor, even if they are in the next room. This technique of inventing negative feedback out of your own head and then reacting to it as if it was real is called "paranoia." Remember this, because it will come up again. And again.

your hips and buttocks into blobs of under-cooked oatmeal. Now, equate these formless clumps with your over-all appeal and human worth! Mutter to whom-ever: "If anyone tried to drive over this ass, they'd break an axle."

Ghastly #4: "Down There"

Q: When it comes to loathing my most intimate parts, isn't it easier to just pretend I don't have any?

Tip

Advanced Tip: For an added boost, invest in a pricey and time-con-suming anti-cellulite regimen; enjoy the false sense of control you get from following a disciplined routine; then call yourself bad names, like "sucker" and "subcutaneous slut" when the ivy extract and sandblaster (etc.) don't work!

A: Easier, maybe. But the most effective, time-tested way to loathe your genitals is to examine them thoroughly while imagining (or remembering) a nun or a nanny telling you that if you keep this up you will go to Hell. Ignore how they feel and forget that they are an organic part of you or that you're sometimes rather fond of them. Scrutinize them as if they were something you turned up in the garden, under a rock.

You may want to single out facets of your genital area to loathe—stubble, labial folds, secretions (smegma! epithelial sloughing!), and odors (see above)—but the most time-saving method (and a wicked thrill to boot) is to get grossed out by all your reproductive organs at once—the holes, the tubes, the fissures and crannies, blood and gore, not to mention the diseases that stalk them and the dark genetic secrets they harbor—and to reject yourself along with them, even though you know you shouldn't.

Booster Tip #1

You can double or triple your self-loathing by attending feminist cultural events like Eve Ensler's *The Vagina Monologues*, at which everyone chuckles condescendingly at women (like you) who sometimes look askance at their vaginas, dismissing them (you) as pathetic, brainwashed by the patriarchy, and benighted!

Booster Tip #2

Take a risk and confide your feelings in a friend. If she secretly feels the same, the two of you will have a great laugh. If she doesn't, she will make you feel like you're in Hell, forced by nuns to spend eternity celebrating vaginas with Eve Ensler.

Master of Female Bodily Self-Loathing: Mo'nique (1967–)

Using her dynamic personality and good humor, Mo'nique urges women to adore their chronic obesity. Her FAT (Fabulous And Thick) beauty pageants on TV reward contestants for losing their self-loathing instead of 150 excess, life-shortening pounds. You, the viewer, get to cheer for another women's pre-diabetic, heart-stopping heft while you struggle to avoid her fate. This casts you in the drama as both a hypocrite and a bit of a killer, and, now that you understand that, you can absorb all the self-loathing that the plus-sizers have shed!

If you are among the minority of female self-loathers who never find their vagina as unnerving as it is fascinating, don't be discouraged: yeast, childbirth, or menopause will come to your rescue.

ONE NEARLY LAST QUESTION

Q: What's the single most annoying thing I can hate about my body if I'm a woman?

A: Angelina Jolie (when she remembers to eat)

BONUS MANTRA

I am strong. I am invincible. I am lying.

UNISEX CHAPTER REVIEW

THREE-QUESTION SPOT QUIZ

Write in as many words as you (honestly) can in each blank below:

I can charm and yet profoundly disgust myself with the following cutsey-poo names* for my intimate parts _____.

Being close to somebody doesn't mean you want them to see your _____.

Just because I hate my _____ doesn't mean I hate myself, only I guess in a way it really does.

***Warning:** Cutesy-poo names will not disgust you if you are *Vagina Monologues* author Eve Ensler.

THIS CHAPTER'S MANTRA

Start by doing what's necessary,
then what's possible, and
suddenly you are hating
how you look
in a monokini.

PART II
THE MATERIAL WORLD

"... IN THE LONG RUN, ORGANIC FOODS, MINIMUM WAGES AND CLEVER MARKETING WON'T SOLVE OUR ESSENTIAL DILEMMA. HOW WILL AMERICA SATISFY BOTH ITS CONSUMERISM AND ITS CORE CONSCIENCE?"

—DANA GOLDSTEIN '06, "THE BROWN DAILY HERALD," APRIL 26, 2007

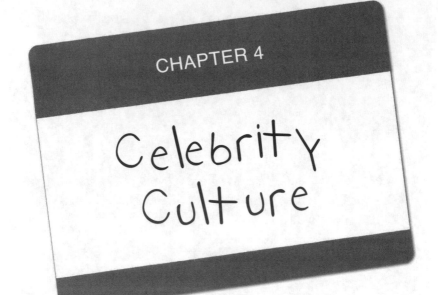

CHAPTER 4

Celebrity Culture

"I sometimes think I've made a whole career of self-loathing."

—*Bobos in Paradise* (2000), David Brooks

IT IS NATURAL to envy famous creatures who loathe themselves more compellingly than you do. What self-loather has not wished to be or to be closer to Robert Downey Jr. when he's using, Nick Nolte when he's drinking, Winona Ryder when she's caught shoplifting, or Angelina Jolie back when she and Billy Bob Thornton were sucking each other's blood? When Philip Seymour Hoffman brought to life a modern sampler of profound self-loathers in *Boogie Nights, Capote, The Savages,* and *Before the Devil Knows You're Dead,* his ability to portray every nuance of self-repulsion—and do it with unprecedented vitality and glee—made him the darling of critics and directors.

Until recently, the closest an ordinary self-loather could get to understanding how celebrities nauseate themselves was to read Cintra Wilson's essay collection: *A Massive Swelling: Celebrity Re-examined as a Grotesque Crippling Disease.* But today your chances of experiencing celebrity self-loathing firsthand are much higher. Reality show celebrity, in which media darlings are created by amateur experts and Viewers Like You, is being replaced by YouTube celebrity, chosen by anyone awake at 3:00 A.M. and too tired to download R. Kelly's *Trapped in the Closet.* The idea, if you can call it one, that anyone with a little self-loathing and a video camera can become a star, should make it easier for you to feel that something is terribly wrong with you if you are not yet famous for drooling when you snore.

THE TABS

Tabloids often cover stories about self-loathing celebrities, but reading them can also boost your own self-hatred, in three big ways:

1. There's something about savoring other people's tragedies and frailties for their entertainment value that excites self-disgust in many decent, hard-working voyeurs. Especially because it's so much fun.

2. Advertisers pay media outlets for "eyeballs," so your interest in a story enlarges its market. When you consume gossip and scandal media, the paparazzi are working to satisfy you, and if a beautiful princess dies trying to escape from them you can rightly consider yourself partly responsible, especially since it didn't stop you from watching her sons grieve.

3. Even if you feel no pangs about your part in hounding celebrities to death, you can always sharpen your self-loathing by tallying up the time you spent watching and gossiping about some scandal when you should have been creating one of your own. (See next page.)

PEOPLE WHO NEED PEOPLE

YOUR QUESTIONS ANSWERED

Q: Did Barbra Streisand and Michael Jackson have their noses whittled down in a series of painful operations because they hated their ethnicity, or because they loved themselves so much they felt they deserved a mainstream audience?

A: Both. A celebrity's job is to keep millions of biased strangers happy. If there's something about their true self that stars fear an audience will reject, they are supposed to lose it or hide it. But the temptation when second-guessing your audience is to get it wrong: to decide, for example, that what's hurting your popularity is your nose—rather than your being a harpy or a pedophile.

CELEBRITY CUT-UPS

Which six of these pop divas were sure that they needed more than just their music to win fans? How many paid doctors to cut their breasts open and fill them with foreign matter? Which of them had her implants removed? Which of them had her implants removed and then signed them and gave them to Jack Osbourne?

Christina Aguilera
Mariah Carey
Jessica Simpson
Lil' Kim
Courtney Love
Kimberly Stewart

Answers:
Signed?—Stewart.
Removed?—Love.
Cut?—All.
All six.
Needed more?—

Tabloid Time Wasters

Sensational Story	Time I Wasted on It in Days
Glamorous bad-girl actress steals actor-stud from girl-next-door actress	____
Winner took steroids, had to relinquish cup	____
Star athlete killed dogs, had to eat crow	____
Androgynous pop star has unconventional childcare methods	____
Catholic priests' childcare methods revealed to be exactly what everybody thought	____
Boy guns down classmates for no reason, poses for camera, commits suicide	____
Man who could not have murdered child beauty queen says he did it	____
Famous dark-skinned athlete who murdered blonde wife, lost celebrity endorsements and rights to confession's profits, arrested for burglary in Vegas	____
Respectable woman operating upscale brothel might release her black book	____
Glamorous, no-longer-naughty star has baby with stolen actor-stud, plus adopts babies all over the world	____
Supreme Court accepts plump blonde bombshell's inheritance case	____
Supreme Court rules in plump bombshell's favor	____
Plump bombshell's son overdoses, dies; she overdoses, dies	____
Many men claim to be her daughter's father and fight over where to bury her; DNA proves the cutest man baby's dad	____

PORN

Q: Now that eXXXplicit sex has gone mainstream, and I can get it in art museums and on my iPhone, can I still loathe myself for needing hardcore porn to get hard (wet)?

A: Yes indeed! And whether you spend your evenings watching reality show contestants eat worms or watching Jenna Jameson eat the things that she eats, choosing crass entertainment over genuine intimacy will eventually excite in you a giant geyser of self-disgust. Unless, of course, you are Paris Hilton. (See Impairment Box, this page.)

Q: When I cruise the porn rack, is there anything I can do to enliven the familiar cruddy sensation of finding myself there?

A: Yes again! Try this reverse angle trick: grab a favorite porn rag, but instead of merely loathing yourself for being

Impairment Box

Annals of the Self-Loathing Impaired

Paris Hilton is one of the few people who loves being a celebrity the way the extraterrestrial vixen Barbarella loved sex: people can exploit or humiliate her however they like with a clear conscience because she is incapable of the shame that so many people on this planet feel. The day her family realized that the widely circulated sex tape of Hilton having it on with boyfriend Rick Salomon was enhancing her market value, they made a deal for a piece of the action and resigned themselves to capitalizing on *1 Night in Paris*, as they would any other celebrity spinoff (except that the profits were demurely earmarked for charity). It's not like sex with Salomon was an emotionally naked event: what Paris delivered was a credible porn performance rather than an intimate moment. And that was no fluke: as long as a camera is on her, Hilton simply does not have a self—either to loathe, or to reveal.

excited by cheesy, desperate sex objects, imagine you ARE a cheesy, desperate sex object. Are you doing it? Good. Now, loathe yourself from (what you imagine is) that cheesy, desperate sex object's point of view as well.

SHOW BIZ

No matter how high you go, there is a self-loathing opportunity for you in show business. Here is a short list of things you can lie awake writhing over (or take drugs to forget) during your Hollywood career:

A POCKET GUIDE FOR HOLLYWOOD SELF-LOATHERS

1. You are a nobody; valets and maître d's send you to Siberia.

2. You are recognized but not by those who count, so you are grossly under-compensated, assigned a lowly parking space, and when a better-paid, better-born star shakes your hand, he looks over your shoulder to see if anyone more interesting is around.

3. You are successful "enough," but not a household name, and although you know fame is a burden you're better off without, you can't stop feeling that you've lost the game.

4. You are fabulously successful and beloved, but your self-loathing turns out to be impervious to the adulation of others.

5. You are fabulously successful and mobbed wherever you go, but the person everyone adores isn't the real you, and you are achingly lonely

and wish you were a "real person," or, if not, at least someone who does something for Africa.

6. You are fabulous-ly successful and adored, but by idiots. Those you really respect aren't returning the favor.

7. You spend years following a guru in search of ego-detachment, and just when you think you're getting close, your pet project dies, and every self-loathing iota of your ego resurfaces instantly!

8. You love your wealth and success, but live in fear of ending up in Polident ads when your star fades.

9. You no longer care what the crowds think of you, but can't forgive yourself for screwing up your relationships with your spouses and kids.

Can ex-child-stars self-loathe?

Ex-child-stars, having played so many differ-ent selves before their identity forms, are likely to be unsure where their own self is, or unable to take it seriously enough to loathe it no matter what they do. Drew Barrymore, Judy Garland, Britney Spears and Lindsay Lohan were all child stars and all druggy, irresponsible hellions. But when can they credit their bad behavior to the noble tradition of self-loathing, and when is it merely the sign of a spoiled brat or a lost soul? (For the verdict, see "Does She or Doesn't She?" Boxes on pages 141 and 124.)

Q: What's the difference between child-stars-gone-wild Britney Spears and Judy Garland?

A: Oh, I don't know: hair clippers, beaver shot, heart, talent?

10. You find yourself on the dais with a score of decrepit former Oscar winners and remember that when you were younger you thought you'd kill yourself rather than be exhibited under glass like an ice-age mummy, at which point you realize that you've gotten so used to feeling some level of self-disgust that one more bout of it hardly seems to merit suicide anymore, which is what you guess maturity means.

Q: Any good advice for a self-loather setting out in show business?

A: If at first you don't succeed, try and try to hide it. That way people (including you) might still mistake you for someone worth knowing.

Q: Do you think I'll ever learn to enjoy loathing myself as much as Jack Nicholson?

A: As a beginner you can never lose by comparing your self-loathing to a celebrity's. If the celebrity, like Jack Nicholson, seems to enjoy it more than you thought possible, you can pick up a lot of tips. If, on the other hand, you think your self-loathing has the celebrity's beat, you're the mack!

See how win-win that is? Try it with any celebrity you like.

Tara and You

Tara Reid's glamorous image appears on a million Web sites, but so do her puckered belly skin and nipple scars. She may not loathe herself over the indecent exposure, but you may feel mildly disgusted with yourself for belonging to a media culture that encourages it.

But, as your question implies, quantity of self-loathing is irrelevant. The point is, celebrities loathe themselves *better* than you do. They are more charming at it and get paid more for doing it and have entourages to help them manage it. Unlike you.

> If you see a famous person you want to meet and don't go up to them, you can feel disgust over how intimidated you are by fame, (too shy, too dull to think of something clever to say).
>
> If you do go and start a conversation, you fear that you have been rude, (disrespectful of others' privacy, a starfucker).

The price of celebrity, however, is steep. Celebrities must appear at televised award ceremonies at least once a year and let everyone watch them lose. Hopefully you will be ready for your HDTV close-up, because when you lose they always give you one, whereas when you win, you can't be guaranteed a close-up unless you cry.

What there should be is an Academy of Self-Loathing Awards ceremony. And if there was, here's who would win what:

THE ACADEMY OF SELF-LOATHING AWARDS

Sexiest portrayal of self-loathing:
Angelina Jolie in *Girl Interrupted*
—Jolie got an Oscar for making self-loathing look incredibly hot, then starred as incredibly-hot-but-silly Lara Croft to experience self-loathing for real.

Most astounding actual self-loathing:
Actor: Mickey Rourke   Actress: Marilyn Monroe
—Whether getting battered to a pulp in the boxing ring or throwing diva fits on set, these two had the good sense to leave the worshipping to their fans.

Most convincing on-screen portrayal of self-loathing:
Actress: Charlize Theron as serial killer Aileen Wuornos in *Monster*
Actor: Nick Nolte in *Affliction.*
—*She* needed to use putty to look depraved.

Most convincing and actual self-loathing comedians:
Richard Pryor, tied with Larry David and Margaret Cho, tied with Sandra Bernhard
—Good comics merely kill. Great comics arrange double suicides.

Best portrayal of show-biz self-loathing in a film script:
Adaptation by Charlie Kaufman
—He even uses the word.

Best self-loathing picture:
Leaving Las Vegas, with Nick Cage
—On a double bill with *Barfly*

Best embodiment of the essence of self-loathing in human form:
Michael Douglas
—No matter how mean his villains are, they always look so allergic to themselves, you almost feel for them.

Best self-loathing line in dramatic media, 21st century:
"Truth? You want truth? I'm a fat fuck from New Jersey."
—Tony Soprano

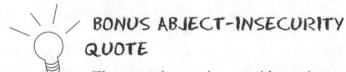

BONUS ABJECT-INSECURITY QUOTE

"I've wanted more than anything to have your respect. The first time I didn't feel it, but this time I feel it, and I can't deny the fact that you like me, right now, you like me!"—Sally Field accepting her second Oscar. (The first one didn't convince her.)

ONE LAST QUESTION

Q: And the Self-Loathing Lifetime Achievement Award goes to . . .

A: Who was Marlon Brando?

Master of Celebrity Self-Loathing: Marylynn Aminrazavi (1961–)

Aminrazavi didn't realize that she was world-renowned for butchering Boyz II Men's "I'll Make Love to You" while lying on the beach and singing along to her iPod until well after her son's video went viral on YouTube. By handling her rather humiliating celebrity with grace, she has helped to usher in an era in which people are not only "famous for 15 minutes," as Pop Art's Andy Warhol predicted, but an age in which you may be famous this very second—close-up, ready or not.

THIS CHAPTER'S MANTRA

All the world's a stage,
upon which
I am
bombing.

CHAPTER 5

The Fashionable Self-Loather

"Fashion is made to become unfashionable."

—Coco Chanel, *Life*, Aug 19, 1957

WHILE CELEBRITY culture produces enough self-loathing for most beginners to work with, what fashion offers is the chance to play with it. Put ruffles on it. Make it work for you. The way you use clothes and accessories can mask self-loathing you're not ready to expose, advertise self-loathing you'd like to be known for, and scramble self-loathing you feel proudly ambivalent about so that no one can distinguish it from your self-love. Besides, like eating, style isn't optional; you have one, like it or not. If you don't either follow fashion or create one of your own, then your statement is "Rip Torn's mug shot."

Fashion's professionals self-loathe by unforgiving standards—their own, and those of peers and colleagues. But to beginners they offer brand-name merchandise—clothes that turn you into an advertisement for the seller's logo. Wearing these offerings lets you show the fashion conscious that you have abjectly entrusted your personal style to, well, somebody with some concept you don't really understand but that seems to be working for others in your milieu. In other words, submitting to branded clothing is a form of self-loathing lite that, if the colors are neutral and the fit is good, can pass for the fashion confidence you loathe yourself for lacking.

But fashion-curious students of self-loathing will want to risk a little—even if it means looking like Bellatrix Lestrange or Boy George. So we will look into alternate options. We will also study a few bad mistakes for their instructional value, visit the dark side of high fashion, and, as always, answer the improbable questions we put in your mouth.

FIRST IMPRESSIONS

First impressions are quick, so make sure that your entire look can transmit everything you want people to know about your self-loathing in one quick line . . . as long as that line is neither "Please, please, please, please like me," or "I feel like Jabba the Hutt in this."

Here is a sampling of . . .

SUITABLE LOOKS TO CHOOSE FROM

Professional: Studied insouciance—Mail-order chinos, old shirt, and soft shoes. A high-priced high school uniform that says: "Inside I'm still that scared, nervous kid I had to bludgeon and dismember to get where I am today."

Advanced: Studied inappropriateness—Narciso Rodriguez jacket (black) worn with a black, long-sleeved mock-turtleneck T-shirt and ponytail says "I'm brave enough to break a rule or two . . . as long as I don't lose the client."

Beginner: Inappropriate insouciance—Red Converse sneakers on a wedding guest says, "I need love so bad that you can count on me to scamper as soon as it's offered." To those paying close attention, it also says, "I know you get turned on by abandonment, and I'm good for that."

Professional: Timeless elegance—Calvin, quality, cashmere and camel's hair, costly and conspicuously inconspicuous say, "Yes, I'm an asshole, but I'm a rich and powerful asshole, and I've learned to live with it."

Advanced: Timeless irony—Olsen twins' high-end grunge if you're rich (but with good skin, great teeth, and an ivy education), "swellegance" if you're struggling (distressed gowns and tuxes worn in full daylight), and if you're middle class, imitate one of the others. All of these looks brag, "I have no class at all!"

Beginner: Elegant irony—something really vulgar from decades ago (fedoras, disco collars, Nancy Sinatra boots, hippie blouses) shouts "I'm hip!" which means you secretly know you're not.

Professional: Pretend gender reversal—Outfits designed by a brilliant friend or Band of Outsiders. Evokes a man-tailored suit on Dietrich, Annie Hall's hat, eyeliner on Johnny Depp. All these say: "Self-loathing? Self-adoring? More 'bi-self-relational.'"

Advanced: Grand gender reversal—There's no better way than a sex swap or a drop of drag to say, "I'm self-loathing and proud!"

Beginner: Pretend grandeur—For women, a little black dress with one vivid detail, a flounce or embroidered hole, says, "I doubt I'd be noticed in *just* a little black dress." For men? Tattoos peeking out from your collar say, "Ask me about my Japanese gangster tat, because I am otherwise as articulate as a fuel pump."

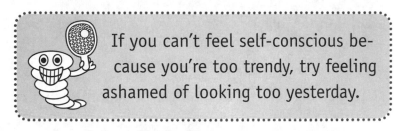

If you can't feel self-conscious because you're too trendy, try feeling ashamed of looking too yesterday.

FASHION MINEFIELD

As usual, self-loathers who attempt to avoid self-loathing rather than display it wittily often defeat themselves. For example, ordinary or plain-looking people who copy celebrity hairdos in the pathetic hope that they will thereby acquire star mojo always end up looking like, well, like they're copying a celebrity's hair in the pathetic hope of looking like a star.

FAMOUS HAIR—'DOS THAT INSPIRED A LEGION OF DON'TS

Elvis Presley's pompadour

The Beatles' bowl haircuts

Farrah Fawcett's side flips in *Charlie's Angels*, the TV series

Bo Derek's blonde cornrows in *10*

Jackie Onassis's beehive

Telly Savalas's bald pate in *Kojak* (aka Bruce Willis)

Yvonne de Carlo's vampire hair as Lily Munster in *The Munsters*

The mullets of Billy Ray Cyrus and Joe Elliott (of Def Leppard)

Madonna's black roots in *Desperately Seeking Susan* (see Inspiration Box, page 187)

Princess Di's corgi cut

The crisscross part of Jennifer Aniston's Rachel in *Friends*

The L Word's portfolio of shags

REGRETTABLE TATS

Although you can now get tattoos that are easier to remove, you still might want to get the old-fashioned kind that you'll regret forever. If so, here are the Top Six Styles of Regrettable Tattoos.

1. "(Summer lover's name) FOREVER!"

2. Image of snake whose head encompasses your genitalia

3. Windows logo

4. "X" on forehead

5. Portrait of Hulk Hogan (or portrait of Hulk Hogan wrestling Godzilla)

6. "I am a telemarketer; pick up the receiver" with arrow pointing to genitals.

And there are, of course, a long list of tattoos in Chinese or Celtic script that say things you didn't mean to say, like, "I put lead in your child's toy," or "All the Celts laugh at me."

DON'TS, DOS, AND DIDS

Leaders and tastemakers who commit fashion crimes are fun to mock: it brings them down to your deplorable level—or even lower. Like U.S. President George W. Bush's vainglorious USAF A-2 flight suit and populist presidential wannabe John Edwards's overpriced haircut, all the fashion "Don'ts" below are fair game.

FOR EACH OF THESE "FASHION DON'TS," NAME ONE HIGH-PROFILER WHO DID

1. DON'T wear four full wands of non-waterproof black mascara on the day you learn that your husband has been unfaithful.

2. DON'T represent the U.S. at a Holocaust memorial wearing a green parka and ski cap when all the other dignitaries are in dark, formal top coats.

3. DON'T wear a pink-and-black St. John's suit to an inquiry about your possibly shady dealings in a famously corrupt Southern state.

4. DON'T wear a sweet pink tie instead of your usual bloody red one to the press conference at which you more-or-less apologize for shooting your friend in the face.

5. DON'T wear a red dress on a diplomatic visit to a country in which only prostitutes wear red.

6. DON'T pretend to be kidnapped, smear yourself with feces, and then let yourself be discovered dressed in a garbage bag.

7. DON'T send high-fashion models in vests and pantaloons made of garbage bags down the runway.

8. DON'T wear a gangster's fedora and trench coat on the courthouse steps after pleading guilty to charges of fraud and conspiracy to bribe officials.

9. DON'T wear a cap that advertises a swank golf club only weeks after pleading guilty to bribing officials with trips to swank golf clubs.

10. DON'T wear some sort of costume that suddenly lets your bare breast pop out in primetime in front of every television camera at the Super Bowl.

11. DON'T wear short skirts without underwear after shaving your pudendum bald, then get out of taxis in front of paparazzi.

Answers:

1. Tammy Faye Bakker reacting to news of husband Jim's weaknesses in 1987; 2. Dick Cheney in January 2005; 3. Hillary Clinton at an April 1994 Whitewater inquiry; 4. Dick Cheney hunting trip with pal Harry Whitington in February of 2006; 5. Pat Nixon in China 1972; 6. Tawana Brawley—Al Sharpton's favorite race case until she confessed her mistreatment was a DIY crime in 1987; 7. Designer Alexandre Herchcovitch at fashion week in New York, 2007; 8. Jack Abramoff at first trial for fraud and attempted bribery in U.S. District Court, Washington DC on January 3, 2006; 9. Jack Abramoff again—this time in Florida soon after; 10. Janet Jackson at 2004 Super Bowl; 11. Britney Spears in December 2006. (See "Does She or Doesn't She?" page 141.)

RESTRAINTS AND REWARDS

Fashion has blurred the line between self-love and self-loathing for centuries, and few can escape, because once a self-hating look becomes fashionable enough, you appear self-loathing if you avoid it. Refuse fashion's mandate and you are likely to be mocked and scorned by (1) the fashion police, (2) alpha mates, and (3) many employers. So, even if you are being literally tortured by your group's beauty standards, the physical pain of mastering the look is usually less than the price of rejecting it.

If you yearn to make the price of social acceptance excruciatingly high in your circle, you can draw inspiration from the past as well as the present.

Why Don't You . . .

Then	Now
—Beautify your lower lip, earlobe, or septum by cutting a hole in it and inserting progressively larger discs of wood until your lip is big enough to serve hors d'oeuvres on?	—Instead of inserting big disks in your cuts, why not try silicone pillows?
—Slash your face and body, then rub ashes into the cuts to make an attractive and spiritually meaningful pattern of scars?	—Express yourself with a tongue stud the size of a gumball or a tattooed image of *The Rape of the Sabine Women* on your back?
—Add a metal ring around your daughter's collarbone each year until her neck is stretched too thin to support her head?	—Wear killer four-inch heels that shrink your Achilles tendons but that make your legs look longer and your feet shorter?
—Wear heavy black cloth on your head in the Arabian desert—bunched into large turbans, hoods, caftans, or veils?	—Wear huge fur coats in the deserts of Los Angeles, or bare your shoulders in the refrigerated ballrooms of Texas?
—Tighten a corset made of wood or iron or whalebone until your lower ribs break?	—Have the fat sucked out of your hips with a long needle?
—Use poisonous belladonna drops to brighten your eyes?	—Get botulism toxin (Botox) injections to smooth your furrowed brow?

QUESTIONS FROM THE FLOOR

Slim blonde woman with clear skin wearing pants of Ingeo, a polymer spun from corn: Why do you focus on the dark and twisty parts of commercial fashion? I mean, yoga clothing is loose and soft, flowing, comfortable. It is kind to the body and to the spirit. When I wear it I feel good about myself!

SL4B: How'd you get in here? Yoga is next door. Shoo! Go away. Christ. Next?

Adorable schlub from either Ohio, Brooklyn, or both: Um, okay. I was just wondering, what should I put on my T-shirt to let people know that I'm less fun than I look?

SL4B: Well, pretty much anything! Corporate and institutional logos, iron-on photos of your pet, ads for failed businesses, slang terms for repulsive sex acts that only a few people can decode, political slogans, sleazy jokes, team logos, jersey numbers, and whatever you want to buy off our website: www.sl4b.com.

Nailed It

Photographer Helmut Newton captured fashion's kinky power to hobble, protect, objectify, and glorify when he posed model Jenny Kapitan in high heels, leg cast and neck brace.

Suburban dumpling who looks 13 and has no idea of how adorable she is: I'm 16 years old and want to become anorexic or bulimic. Can I do it just by looking at pictures of Kate Moss?

SL4B: My dear: Kate Moss's image has appeared on over 300 magazine covers all over the world. But have you ever visited a mall in Mississippi? Ohio? Omaha? Those women have seen Kate Moss's picture, too, but do any of them look like they would turn down a happy meal or throw up after wolfing one down? No. They look like fertility goddesses. Sumo wrestlers. If Kate Moss or even Barbie had the power to make girls like you starve themselves until they grow fur, obesity in America would be herstory.

Bulimic wannabe (near tears): I have so much trouble vomiting! What can I do . . . ?

SL4B: If you really want to go bulimic, your best bet is to move somewhere like Manhattan or zip code 90210—image-making centers where staying thin as a credit card is a must. In such ferociously competitive places, Kate Moss isn't a "role model"; Kate Moss is the job description. And if you want the job—if you want to be paid mogul money, to be invited everywhere, to be desired and forgiven for your little problems with cocaine and cool-but-elusive men—and you don't have the bones or the genes du jour, I promise that in a matter of months you will either lose your appetite or want to throw up.

Bicoastal metrosexual in retail promotion: Which clothing line is best for my rugged self-loathing lifestyle: Alexander McQueen or L.L. Bean?

SL4B: Both are great! L.L. Bean's clunky clothing will reassure everyone that, even though your nails are manicured, you have no taste, and a McQueen man-skirt, whether worn in the woods or with bagpipes, will show everyone that you have no fear.

Famously self-loathing Desperate Housewife Felicity Huffman's free-floating thought bubble: I see men in greasy toupees and women who wear big swooshes of green eyeliner and enough foundation to stucco a bungalow, but they don't seem to loathe their self-presentation as much as I loathe mine. Why is that?

SL4B: When people embrace their own ugliness with gusto, their disgust with themselves becomes invisible to us. It's when people seem to be afraid of being ugly that they can get scary. [See (again) Donatella Inspiration Box, page 204.]

Worst-dressed contender: Should I try to get on a makeover show like *Queer Eye for the Straight Guy,* so I can be mocked and humiliated by millions, or should I concentrate on having my fashion sense derided by people I respect?

SL4B: You can light this candle at both ends, but the contempt of genuine experts gives off a more mellow glow. Also, it smells more like Clive Christian No. 1 and less like Raid.

The Skin Game

PETA has sponsored a series of ads that offer women a whirlwind self-loathing opportunity. They all feature beautiful naked women who urge you to "turn your back on fur." Sadie Frost, actress, fashion designer, and Jude Law's ex-wife, has such a lovely curve to her back and posterior, that beholding it makes you cry aloud, "God, that ass would look good in a sable coat!" or, "An ass like mine would look a whole lot better in a sable coat," or even, "I bet if Jude Law gave me a sable coat, I'd kiss his ass." In any case, you'll get to feel all guilty and wicked, even if the closest you'll ever get to a fur coat is petting your pug.

Husband of worst-dressed: I want to dress so that wherever I go everyone feels embarrassed for me. How can I do it without being mistaken for "ironic" or "hip"?

SL4B: Sorry, in most circles you no longer can. But try showing up unexpectedly at a fundraiser in a knock-off of Joan Rivers's latest Oscar frock.

Master of Fashion Self-Loathing: Charles Robert Darwin (1809–1882)

By uncovering our animal ancestry, Darwin helped to establish the philosophical basis for animal rights. Thanks to him, we can now hate ourselves for wearing pelts, leathers, feathers, and industrially harvested wool ripped from the flesh of our relatives.

ONE LAST QUESTION

Q: Which looks more self-loathing: a grunge look, goth, punk, prostitot, Ugly Betty, *gangsta bling, or an overdone Lacroix-Gucci-*Absolutely Fabulous *Chanel-Goes-Plaid kind of statement?*

A: When in doubt, best to go for the underpants-on-the-head look.

THIS CHAPTER'S MANTRA

Behind the clouds the sun is hiding—from me, because this outfit makes my ass look lumpy.

CHAPTER 6

Food for Self-Loathing

"There, but for a typographical error, is the story of my life."

—Dorothy Parker, when told by her host that guests in another room were "ducking for apples"

IN THE OLD DAYS the saying went, "You are what you eat." Today, we say, "You loathe what you eat AND you are what you eat, so you loathe what you are!"

Food is a most versatile tool for self-loathers. You can use it as a stand-alone, or combine it with other self-hating devices. Your bodily self-loathing, familial self-loathing, and self-loathing-on-a-date skills will all start to pay off when you sit down to dinner, particularly in a restaurant.

They will serve you well, too, if you decide to "drink your dinner" in a bar night after night because your new car is a lemon, your novel was rejected again, and you never were any good to anybody anyhow.

This chapter will cover the rudiments of gustatory self-loathing, omitting many important aspects of self-loathing food preparation and presentation, a topic definitively covered in Amy Sedaris's instant classic, *I Like You: Hospitality Under the Influence.* Any wisdom not found there can be gleaned from the age-old saying: "When life gives you lemons, make whiskey sours."

DIETS

We begin with dieting because it is the best way to simultaneously express, feed, and style your self-loathing. Let's explore some well-known diets and styling tips on how to use them.

THE ANCIENT-RELIGIOUS-CUSTOMS DIET

Like "Thou shalt not cook the calf in its mother's milk," or "Pork is unclean," or "If alcohol touches your sinful lips you'll burn in Hell."

Style Tip: Break the ban and suffer the displeasure of your god, or inconvenience everyone at a dinner  party with your request for peanut butter instead of shrimp kebabs. You can also order special meals on airlines and feel horribly exposed when the steward bearing your tray shouts "Halal!" singling you out as a potential terrorist on a crowded airplane.

THE PERSONAL-MORAL-CREDO DIET

"I don't eat animals"; "I don't eat products of animal husbandry (like eggs and dairy)"; "I don't eat factory-raised meat or over-fished species"; "I don't eat anything that wasn't produced sustainably"; "I don't eat anything genetically modified, out of season, not organic, out of my foodshed, or produced by exploited labor"; "I don't eat anything smarter than I am."

Style Tip: Your moral inferiors have words for people like you, and they aren't "great guest." Stop loathing yourself on behalf of the pig long enough to empathize with your poor dining companions. If you marinate your hatred of culinary sin in disgust at your own self-righteousness, you can make your tough moral fiber into something much more digestible.

THE DOCTOR'S-ORDERS DIET

As in, "You're allergic to wheat," or, "Cut down on the salt (fat, sugar, alcohol, caffeine, nuts)," or, "Don't eat anything 5 hours before you go to bed."

Style Tip: In lay jargon this means, "You'll never dine out with civilized people again," and though you're not to blame, you're now a pathetic gastronomical cripple. Console yourself by defying your doctor, and then you can blame yourself later when you feel like something the cat spat up.

THE LIVE-FOREVER DIET

Scientific research suggests that you, like mice, might live a lot longer if you eat about as much as a mouse eats.

Style Tip: Getting proper nutrition while on that diet of yours means planning each meal with a digital scale and nutrient calculator, discussing calorie counts with other people on longevity diets, and doing Sudoku puzzles in an effort to keep your brain as fit as your body. In other words, you may live forever, but as something resembling a lab rat, and you will never dine out with civilized people again. You're better off loathing yourself for breaking this diet than loathing yourself for being mortal.

THE WACKY, QUACKY DIET

The best of these were designed for people in another climate, culture or century, in places where sprouts, seaweed, and gassy legumes were all you could get.

Style Tip: Figure out witty ways to apologize often for your diet's chief side effect . . . deafening flatulence.

THE WEIGHT-LOSS DIET

Weight-loss regimes, whether for reasons of health or vanity, are too numerous to list, but see the diet "Menu" below for the major categories. . . .

Style Tip: All weight-loss regimes have one great virtue, namely that within a year of reaching your target weight most of you will wake up and realize to your delight that you are going to get to diet again! Once more you'll have to locate your base-line bodily self-loathing and kick it up a few notches until it ceases to be bearable. (**Super Tip:** Try abandoning the familiar phrase, "I wonder how I'd look in a muumuu," or the more upscale version, "Gosh! I look like William Shatner in a pup tent!" and replace it with something a bit more rude, like, "Gack! Even I wouldn't do me!")

Once your will is roused, your diet can begin. Spend the next weeks or months thinking continuously about what you will eat next and when, experiencing a pleasant buzz of intellectual devolution ("Hey, get this! I responded to the sound of that can of tuna popping open exactly like Boots!"). Finally, when you see a story about earthquake refugees on TV and all you can think about is, "I wonder what they get to eat in those CARE packages," you have at last become an entertainment to yourself and others.

YOUR QUESTIONS ANSWERED

Q: Is there any one diet you can recommend?

A: Nearly all diets that work ask you to reduce your calorie count (stay hungry), exercise more (get sore), drink a lot of water (bloat up), and take supplements (trying not to choke). That is, they all make you sorry to be you.

A MENU OF DIETS FOR SELF-LOATHERS (AND OTHERS)

Diet (a): Cut out a food type you love, like meat, fat, or carbs.

Diet (b): Go on diet "(a)," but indulge yourself once a week to fool your body into thinking it isn't starving

The Harris-Lead-Bullet Diet

A girls' school headmistress, and strict disciplinarian, Jean Harris became romantically involved with *The Complete Scarsdale Medical Diet* author, Dr. Herman Tarnower. When he broke it off with her, she later testified, she went to his home intending to kill herself but killed him "accidentally" instead, which was so distressing that suicide slipped her mind. As she did her 11 years behind bars for murder, Harris learned to detest her former prudishness and self-absorption, becoming a model prisoner who helped many less fortunate women. . . . And she stopped obsessing about her weight.

and to intensify your torment by reminding you regularly of what you're missing.

Diet (c): Live on lemon juice with maple syrup, cayenne pepper, vitamins, and laxative tea (the "master cleanse" diet) until your brain digests itself and your worries are over.

GORGING

When a yen for oral gratification conflicts with character goals like self-restraint, gorging is a quick way to fatten up your self-disgust. Try to confuse food and love, and remember: you can't get enough.

Q: What do I do when my stomach gets full?

A: Do not listen to it. If your tongue wants another brew or your teeth want to crunch another Frito, go for it. Ask yourself: why would they sell ice cream in half gallons if that wasn't the ideal portion?

 Professionals already know: the same technique can be easily applied to psychoactive drugs, sex, gambling, and shopping, and with similarly spectacular results.

PURGING

When dieting is too slow and dreary a way to prepare for another moment of gorging, dedicated self-loathers turn themselves inside out and spew forth something pungent and messy. Try it. Seeing your self-revulsion so quickly and so vividly expelled will give you the confidence to try self-loathing again soon. Vomiting (especially in the street or on a pair of $1,200 shoes), laxatives, and high colonics all replace an uncomfortable fullness with delightful vacancy, accompanied by ample evidence of how foul you are behind your mask of effortless sophistication, corporate competence, or street-cred.

Q: Know any way to get it off my breath?

A: Not really. But you raise a good point: nothing brings out the health and happiness police like the reek of bulimia. At least three and a half million people sustain sports injuries each year, yet no one warns you to shun the gym or the ski lift. But if you show any hint of an eating disorder, you will be smothered with concern by people who don't understand you. So if you aren't making yourself throw up out of self-loathing, you will soon be persuaded to loathe yourself because you made yourself throw up. This downward spiral, un-checked, can lead to a fate like Karen Carpenter's (see Inspiration Box, this page).

Q: I like to eat a balanced diet and control my portions. I find it gives me more energy to loathe myself for the important things, like falsifying lab results to get grant money, blackballing people who threaten to expose me, etcetera. Are you sure that you want people to spend their energy

Poster-Thin Girl

Singer and drummer Karen Carpenter died of cardiac arrest failure at the age of 32 early in 1983, after a long history of eating disorders. Years of boosting her metabolism with thyroid meds and purging with laxatives had literally broken her heart. Because she was a pop music legend, yet considered "wholesome," her death made eating disorders both visible and respectable, and people finally realized that while loathing your body is all well and good, when a girl looks in the mirror and thinks her skeleton looks fat, she has a body-image problem.

vomiting and defecating when there are so many better ways to achieve self-hatred?

A: In your case, frankly, yes.

FORAGING

Very often, eating means shopping, and here again you will be able to use all of your hard-won self-castigating techniques. The marketing of food is after all designed to induce self-betrayal, to get you to buy more than you need, especially of the wrong things, like glucose, polypropylene, antibiotics, and snob appeal. If you fight the sell, you will have a tedious experience. Give in, and you will feel shame.

Build your self-loathing tolerance with these . . .

FOOD SHOPPING EXERCISES FOR SELF-LOATHERS

1. Buy bargain foods that turn out to be inedible. Baked goods marked "0 carbs" are a safe bet. Throw them away unfinished and feel guilty, rooked.

2. Fall in love with a brand of cookie that comes with more protective packaging than a laptop. Think of the landfill you're clogging every time you enjoy one and tell yourself it's worth it, but don't believe yourself.

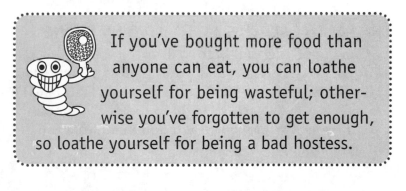

If you've bought more food than anyone can eat, you can loathe yourself for being wasteful; otherwise you've forgotten to get enough, so loathe yourself for being a bad hostess.

3. Come home without the thing you went shopping for. Like your brain.

4. Forget how to tell if a fish is fresh or toxic. Serve it to guests, then stay up all night accusing yourself of poisoning them.

5. Drop a jar of spaghetti sauce in the supermarket. Attention Shoppers! Klutz on Aisle Four!

6. Think about killing the lonely old lady in front of you who is telling the cashier all about her hateful grandchildren in Decatur. What's wrong with you?

7. Keep the whole line waiting while the cashier runs a price check. Now you're no better than that lonely old lady.

8. Forget to get singles to tip the delivery boy. Ditz.

9. Blow the delivery boy. It's the least you can do, lacking singles.

DINING OUT WITH CIVILIZED PEOPLE

Although eating alone, like drinking alone, provides a great workspace for self-abuse, it's even easier when you eat and drink in public. Both activities are rich in potential missteps that will make you writhe with regret in the morning. Here are a few suggestions to get you started.

THE SELF-LOATHER'S GUIDE TO FINE DINING

Start drinking well before dinner so that you can more than amuse those at your table and entertain everyone else in the restaurant as well. Don't make them guess what you'd like to do to Jude Law: announce it to the world. While you're at it, tell them what you did to the delivery boy.

If your plate is an elaborate fantasia made of solidified clam juice, powdered sea urchin, and pumpernickel ice cream with micro shiso leaves, hate it! Hate the people who like it and hate yourself for not being one of them! Make all this clear by announcing that you had a better time on jury duty and laughing until your imported stout comes out of your nose.

When your well-padded sister-in-law says that cows used to graze on her new country property in Tuscany, mutter loudly enough for her to hear, "They still do." Help her learn English by explaining that here in the U.S. the word for her anchovy appetizer is "bait."

Return from the restroom with a paper toilet-seat protector dangling down the back of your slacks and announce with a glamorous flourish, "I have returned!" Smile for the camera phone.

At a high-end restaurant with a tenderhearted friend, order the foie gras. Then find fault with it and send it back. Get bratty when friend rebukes you, then defensive and mean. Let friend pick up the check. Watch yourself do all this and wonder what your problem is.

Spill something, preferably red, all over Russell Crowe.

When choosing the restaurant, pick something too expensive, too hard to get into, too far, too loud, too pretentious, too tacky, too dark, too bright, too yesterday. And be sure to apologize for it all night.

When companions warn you not to order seafood on Monday,

Tip

Advanced tip: Always include yourself in the spill zone.

Professional tip: Attempt to help victim remove stain with club soda and pour way too much of it on victim's loins.

or anything with the word "surprise" in it, order it anyway; hate it; eat off their plates instead.

Bring a child to an adult restaurant with the innocent intention of teaching it table manners in situ. When child begins wilding and you are asked to take it home, realize you should have remained a virgin.

Get a bit frantic flagging down a waiter for your check, only to have your hysteria exposed when he points to where he put it 15 minutes ago. Accuse him of hiding it.

If you're diligent, you can self-loathe just by thinking about food inappropriately, like on a mountaintop where you're supposed to be focusing on Being and Nothingness ("Great: I'm as deep as an ice cream sandwich"), or even during a memorial service that's to be followed by a large buffet ("A great human being is gone; and all I can think about is a cheese puff").

After completing this book you will be able to loathe yourself in a food-connected way wherever food is served, sold, or prepared, including your very own kitchen.

TEST YOURSELF

Q: Which is better fodder for self-loathing, letting a maître d' seat you in the most Siberian corner of a four-star restaurant, or recommending an overpriced, second-class eatery to people you'd like to impress?

A: Whichever one refuses to accept your credit card and costs more cash than you have on you.

Q: Does vomiting from stage fright count as a form of purging?

A: Only if the show you're in is an eating contest.

Q: If I stuff myself to bursting with celery and cucumbers, does that count as a diet or gorging?

A: It counts as dieting, but cheating.

Master of Gustatory Self-Loathing: Edward E. Mason, M.D., Ph.D. (1921–)

In the mid-'60s, Dr. Edward Mason replaced body-punishing intestinal bypass surgery with the lower-impact gastric bypass (stomach stapling). Fifteen years later, he began promoting the Vertical Banded Gastroplasty (VBG), a surgical procedure that has far fewer side effects. Thanks to him, those of us panicked about our morbid obesity can literally tie our stomachs into knots over it.

ONE LAST QUESTION

Q: What do you call someone whose diet harms no living thing?

A: Dead.

THIS CHAPTER'S MANTRA

Eat, drink, and
be sorry.

PART III
INTERACTIVE
SELF-LOATHING

"I WOULD NEVER WANNA BELONG TO ANY CLUB THAT WOULD HAVE SOMEONE LIKE ME FOR A MEMBER. THAT'S THE KEY JOKE OF MY ADULT LIFE IN TERMS OF MY RELATIONSHIPS WITH WOMEN."

— "ANNIE HALL" (1977), WOODY ALLEN

CHAPTER 7

Self-Loathing Sex!

"What am I really, a little dilettante, or a great big donkey?"

—Wanda von Dunajew in *Venus in Furs* (1870), Leopold von Sacher-Masoch's masochistic classic.

THE BIG QUESTION beginning self-loathers always ask about sex and love is: are they inextricably entwined or mutually exclusive?

The answer is that they're both, and more, depending. But the uncertainty about how sex and love interpenetrate—the "if" and "should" of affection, empathy, attachment, longing, and lust—makes for a whirl of internal conflict that keeps a self-loather's relationships fascinating long after they are over—and even before they begin.

Because it is so easy and common to have sex without love and love without sex, each has its own chapter. Each will offer the beginner opportunities to apply lessons learned, because you'll find that pretty much any sneering attitudes about yourself you have mastered thus far will become more exciting in the company of an intimate partner—or two.

Sex offers so many ways to explore your self-loathing that you'll want to have sex—and have it often—for that reason alone. In this chapter we'll look at how self-disgust can make sex interesting before, during, and after, then investigate ways that self-loathers can locate suitable partners to suffer with.

BEFORE

Because combining self-loathing with sexuality causes many beginners feel like a used bar rag, they worry that it makes them unattractive to others. So the first question is:

Q: How can self-loathing be sexy?

A: The short answer is, "Easily." Here are but a few of the techniques you can try:

1. Pornitude. Bursting out of a cake dressed in three feathers, assuming the mating positions of lower vertebrates, and smiling lasciviously while growling "Meow," all signal that you are eager to compensate for your many other inadequacies by performing certain favors until your jaw falls off, dignity be damned. Many people find that message unbelievably arousing.

2. Guilt. Guilty sex also has its avid fans. Whether wronging a god, a mate or just your own better judgment, unholy feelings of thrilling badness can glamorize sexual excitement the way black leather tarts up a motorcycle club. In fact, for many self-loathers sex without guilt is like a balloon without air: still a balloon, but nothing anyone would bother twisting into a dachshund.

3. Hard work. Sexual self-loathing can also be sexy if you *make* it sexy. Lose the idea that sex is "natural" and requires no intervention. Insecure about your looks? Try blindfolding your partner or wearing a paper bag over your head. (Be creative—decorate your bag with a photo of J. Lo, George Clooney, or, if your partner is an intellectual, the book jacket of a first edition of *Ulysses!*) Similarly, if you think you're stupid, make your intellectual self-contempt appealing by pumping up to get that Hulk Hogan look. If you are appalled by your forbidden sexual desires and needs, be patient; you'll eventually find someone just as tortured to kink around with, and the mutual sense of relief and repulsion is likely to be embarrassingly emetic.

If you refuse to sleep with people just because you're extremely attracted to them, you're wasting your youth (a once-in-a-lifetime-opportunity, the club's cover fee), and you'll hate yourself for it.

If you do sleep with them, you can loathe yourself for being decadent (an adulterer, Sienna Miller).

But, to continue: There are many more ways to make self-loathing alluring, as we will see.

So: please don't worry about self-loathing damaging your sex appeal. From the worshippers of Marilyn Monroe and Anna Nicole Smith to the cults of Tommy Lee and Che Guevara, people have chased most passionately after self-loathers who are running away from themselves—and who look good doing it.

DURING

The next anxiety that plagues beginners when they try to mix sex and self-loathing is . . .

Q: Will it turn me off?

A: All indicators suggest that, on the contrary, people who feel bad about themselves—and especially people who feel bad about themselves for having sex—seem to enjoy it as much as or more than people who, while writhing and grunting and screaming bloody murder or sighing and gasping like a dying flounder, believe they're wonderful, adorable creatures having a lovely time.

Q: Can my partner help me enjoy my self-loathing?

A: Mostly by increasing it. For example, here are . . .

TEN THINGS YOU CAN ASK YOUR PARTNER TO SAY THAT WILL MAKE YOU FEEL INADEQUATE IN BED

1. Faster. (Or slower.)

2. Try to pick up my rhythm. . . .

3. That's funny; usually I like the way it tastes.

4. You've done this before . . . right?

5. Hey, would you mind if your best friend joined us?

6. And I thought *I* was bad in bed.

7. Do you ever come?

8. Wake me up when you're finished.

9. Was that it?!?

10. Next!

Q: What if my partner insists on being too reassuring, attentive, and appreciative?

A: Don't count on your partner to make you suffer. You can . . .

APPALL YOURSELF IN BED WITH ANY OF THESE PRE-TESTED SPELL-BREAKERS

1. While rolling over, accidentally get a piece of your partner's flesh caught under your weight-bearing hand, knee, or arm so that they yelp and squeal in pain. Make it worse by apologizing excessively or saying "Don't be such a sissy," instead of kissing it better.

2. Enter an orifice by mistake, or notice that an unusual orifice has been entered, and mistakenly assume it was on purpose but say nothing until afterwards. Either way, shock and awe is likely to ensue, leaving you feeling off-color and off-base. [This approach was allegedly perfected by gynecologist David Hager, President Bush's advisor to the FDA on reproductive policy, and his (now ex) wife, Linda Davis. In 2005, she told *The Nation* that he often forced himself on her while she slept: "He would say, 'Oh, I didn't mean to have anal sex with

you; I can't feel the difference,' And I would say, "Well then, you're in the wrong business!"]

3. Find self unable to undo an undergarment fastening after many suave (then increasingly frantic) efforts, so that you appear inexperienced and uncoordinated—especially if it's your own. (Getting an arm caught or head stuck while removing a shirt or sweater works well, too, especially in a sleeping loft or car where head clearance is limited.)

4. While making love standing up, drop partner or fall off.

5. Bash head on headboard. Hard.

6. While going to kiss partner, collide with partner's nose so hard it bleeds.

7. Choke on partner's pot and cough for several minutes while your eyes turn red, your throat bulges out like an iguana's, and you pretend it isn't happening.

8. Go bone dry or limp after an effort at sexual intimacy has started, but well before it's over. Pretend it isn't happening.

9. Fail to maintain interest in partner during The Act. Whether you fake your way through this one or jump up and shout, "I can't go through with this!" and run from the room, you will not be pleased with yourself.

Seal the Deal Tip: The trick in every case is not to go, "Hey, that sucked!" and move on, the way self-loathing-impaired people do, but to go "Aw geez, I suck." Don't forget to run instant replays of your gaffes in the sports bar of your mind for hours, even days. Which brings us to . . .

AFTER

Many practitioners like to do their self-loathing after sex rather than before or during. This can be done via the so-called "divine judge method"—attending sexually restrictive churches and mosques or sneaking home, getting caught, and lying to a person to whom you've promised your fidelity. (Sneaking home and *not* lying when caught is also popular. Less so the Woody Allen method of being already at your lover's home when the sneaking begins. See "Does He or Doesn't He?" next.)

In one of the strangest cases of self-loathing deficiency on record, director and humorist Woody Allen, famous for styling his every insecurity and self-doubt into absurdist and Freudian jokes, claimed to feel no guilt over an affair that destroyed his family and outraged most of his fans. His romance was with Soon-Yi Previn, then 19 years old and the adopted daughter of his long-time lover, Mia Farrow. Allen and Farrow had three children—two adopted and one biological— so his teenaged lover was technically his children's sister, and then, after he married her, his children's mother-in-law as well. . . . "There's no downside to it," he told *Time* Magazine. "The only thing unusual is that she's Mia's daughter. But she's an adopted daughter and a grown woman. I could have met her at a party or something."

What party—her prom? Verdict: Rationales aside, it's hard to believe that Allen felt no guilt. It seems more likely that he felt it, but loved it too much to label it properly. After all, when asked once if he thought sex was dirty, his famous reply was, "Only if it's done right."

Some lucky sex addicts can achieve postcoital self-loathing simply by having an orgasm! Maybe you can, too. How? When you climax your synapses fill with spurts of dopamine (the neurotransmitter for addiction). If you can get your dopamine overload to trigger a surge in prolactin (the hormone that bitch-slaps the feel-good areas of your brain), your high will turn into a crash, and, bingo!—your bedmate turns into a toad.

Q: If I combine some kind of sexual guilt with the hormone cocktail you just described, will I die of joy?

A: Well, not right away.

Q: What's the quickest and easiest way to disgust myself after an orgasm?

A: Have them all alone.

Q: What's the most vivid way?

A: Have them with strangers in a ditch.

Q: And the way to produce the longest-lasting memories of my post-orgasmic remorse?

A: Have them with close relatives, enemies of your people—or Soon-Yi.

For advanced players who want to max out their post-orgasmic self-loathing, here's . . .

THE 12-STEP PROGRAM

Step 1. Silently observe: "Oh damn (shit, Jesus), here I am: back to the real me."

Step 2. Retreat into hateful self.

Step 3. Refuse partner's attempt at consolation by shaking your head and pleading, "Don't . . . "

Step 4. Say to partner waiting for you to say "I love you," "I really love yyy . . . your roommate." (Laugh.)

Step 5. Hate self for hurting partner's feelings.

Step 6. Start obsessing about someone you once wanted passionately who didn't want you (unlike current partner).

Step 7. Leave abruptly, hurting partner's feelings some more, or apologize insincerely without meeting partner's eyes.

Step 8. Wonder why in God's name (why in hell, why the fuck) you're like this.

Step 9. Have a cigarette and hate self for not quitting.

Step 10. Lie awake until dawn thinking of how great the relationship could be if you weren't such a self-defeating jerk (duplicitous snake, narcissistic swine), then sleep until noon.

Step 11. Wake up feeling vaguely guilty.

Step 12. And horny.

(Repeat as often as desire allows)

HOOKING UP

Once confident that self-loathing can produce a sex life full of passion and incident, beginners are ready to tangle with prospective partners. Those seeking "real" relationships may skip to the chapter on love and commitment, but dating self-loathers, or DSLs, who are just looking for somebody to burn out their dopamine synapses with, will do best to start with the sort of people whose mental state they understand best—self-loathing others, or SLOs.

Some DSLs are born with natural SLO-dar; they have a sixth sense for signs of self-directed doubt, disapproval, and disgust in others, even when those signs are masked by Prada suits, G-unit T-shirts, or a façade of serene, joyful calm, complete with Livestrong bracelet. The rest of us have to use trial and error and crude guides, like the following.

SELF-LOATHER-SEEKING-SELF-LOATHER PICKUP LINES AND WHY THEY WORK (UNISEX)

Line: I'm not trying to pick you up, but if I were, I'd probably say something dumb like this.

Mechanics: If the prospect bites, you've established that you say dumb things to which the prospect tacitly agrees that he/she is dumb enough to respond. You have found an SLO.

Line: Are you as tired of rotgut roadhouse sex as I am?

Mechanics: However much irony clouds this drawled query—and the more the better—anyone who answers is clearly an SLO, and one who is open to your B-movie fantasy of moral degeneracy.

Line: I'll show you my rejected screenplay, if you don't show me yours.

Mechanics: Failure confessed and shame sought. Even a nibble to this one confirms an SLO twosome.

Line: Hey! I have a big mole just like yours, only someplace not just anybody can see it.

Weird Science

Born Erik James Horvat-Markovic, the man now known as "Mystery, the World's Greatest Seducer" was pursuing a magician's career in nightclubs when he discovered that inducing quick little hits of mild self-loathing in beautiful women made it easier to get them into bed. The technique succeeds, he theorizes, because females are biologically "programmed" to mate with males of superior social standing, and the "neg," or mildly amusing put-down, by positioning seducers above their "targets" helps put females in the mood for "replication," aka mating. It's hard to imagine his technique works, but to the extent that it does, many of us may owe our lives to blips of self-loathing that got our mothers into a reproductive mood.

Mechanics: This gross-out sets the stage for the sort of sex in which self-loathing is shared, accepted, and enjoyed—a come-on to which only a fun-loving partial SLO will respond, though they are regrettably rare.

Line: Something tells me you deserve me.

Mechanics: Is this a threat of punishment or a promise of reward? Whatever it means, SLOs will want to know you better.

Instead of manipulating a date into a one-down position, you might want to find an SLO who is already there. If you are on a first date with a possible SLO, and you want a better idea of whether or not your date is squirming inside as much as you are, look for these subtle "tells":

SLO DETECTOR

—forced laughter

—bragging and name-dropping

—compulsive hand-washing

—long tirades about how Kurt Cobain revealed the grungy self-hatred beneath the corn syrup ooze of commercial pop

—long tirades

—long silences

—sobbing

—apologies for sobbing

—apologies for living

—pessimistic come-ons, like, "Oh, let's get this farce over with and just go have sex so we'll have something in common to regret"

Q: Can I use the Internet to seek SLOs for sex?

A: Because the Internet is something of a hall of mirrors (see Inspiration Box, page 108), you run the risk of attracting someone who's self-loathing-impaired. To keep that risk to a minimum, try one of the following approaches.

ONLINE DATING FOR SELF-LOATHERS— SCREENING OUT THE CHAFF

1. Post a picture of a manatee and describe yourself as pudgy, needy, and underachieved. Say you're irritatingly ambitious because you're trying to fill a gaping pit in your soul where mindless self-acceptance should probably be. Add that every night

for weeks you have been reading a book called *Self-Loathing for Beginners*—for fun. Sensitive self-loathers go gonzo for self-deprecation, especially if you don't really look like a manatee.

2. Use some model's picture and say you're creative, rich, generous; you love sports (if female), shopping (if male), collecting art, enjoying fine wines; and are looking to share your mansions around the world with someone who can handle sensual pleasure and unlimited social access to power. Add that you're looking for someone who is not like you at all. A true self-loather will detect your irony and swoon.

3. Get a dog. Put its picture up. If it gets a date, go along to meet the one other person out of billions who has resorted to this desperate measure out of self-loathing and despair.

 N.B. Professional self-loathers don't date: they get entangled with their new love objects on the sly and out of the public eye, either on a movie set while still involved with someone else, or else in broom closets, deserted conference rooms, or while giving the babysitter a lift home.

TWO BEGINNERS' QUESTIONS FROM THE FLOOR

Well-toned divorcée in riding boots with herpes sore: Is it a good idea to skip contraception when I am sleeping with lots of interesting people?

SL4B: Nothing short of running your sports car off the road into a hard object announces your indifference to your own worth better than your eagerness to stake your life and health on a fleeting sexual thrill. But, stylistically, a death wish isn't everything. In fact, flaunting your self-contempt by riding bareback is the sure mark of a novice. Those with a more evolved style use contraception every time and berate themselves for being cautious and considerate about something as savage as sex.

Cocky wiseass with stubble: Will you have sex with me if I buy your book?

SL4B: No, but I'll want to, which is equally degrading.

Guess Who?

Thomas Montgomery, a working man from a small town in upstate New York, courted and fell in love with a pretty young woman he met online by posing as his own son. When a co-worker of Montgomery's told the girl her fantasy boy's true age and then began courting her himself, Montgomery shot him dead. Before he began his 20-year sentence, Montgomery learned that the pretty young woman whose love he killed for was really a middle-aged mother posing as her daughter. As bizarre as these virtual relationships seem, they are typical of the ones self-loathers have when they try to impersonate someone they feel is less undesirable than they are.

ONE LAST QUESTION

Q: What is the single most common cause of self-loathing besides waking up next to a stranger—again?

A: Waking up to find the stranger gone—again.

Master of Sexual Self-Loathing: Alfred Charles Kinsey (1894–1956)

Before Kinsey's famous report, millions of Americans loathed themselves for being sexually deviant. After his studies showed that there was no benchmark of normalcy to deviate from, Americans were finally able to loathe themselves for feeling sexually deviant even though there isn't any such thing, just like Germans or the French.

THIS CHAPTER'S MANTRA

An ounce of
prevention
is worth more
than I am.

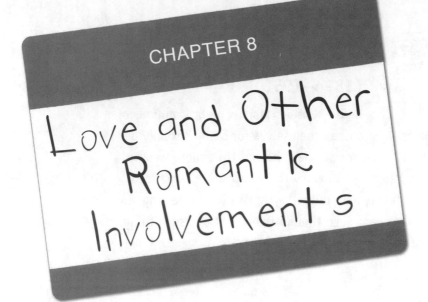

CHAPTER 8

Love and Other Romantic Involvements

"Too strong a love upsets the organism in all its depths—and what rises to the surface is merely nauseating."

—*Querelle de Brest* (1947), Jean Genet

THE MOST storied combination of love and self-loathing is romantic love, an obsessive desire for someone dead, unavailable, or, best of all, way too good for you. Because worshipping someone who makes you feel as worthless as a blob of old gum stuck beneath a discarded chair in a Tennessee dumpster is one of the most wonderful feelings in the world, it is rightfully prized by lovers high and low. Yet it is not the only way love and self-loathing can feed each other. Failing to love those who adore you is always a good excuse to despise yourself, as is the pounding your ego takes when a person or fan club that once thought the world of you suddenly takes it all back.

Note that love need not be sexual to toss you into an emotional abyss:

—You can be disgusted with yourself for sabotaging your mate just to keep your beloved from winning a fellowship abroad;

—You can feel like a fraud for bedding your mate the way Abraham Lincoln did his wife, Mary Todd—while yearning wretchedly for others.

—And, of course, you can loathe yourself for being so damn in love with yourself you can't love anyone else, not even Brangelina.

But doormat or beast, a drop or two of self-inflicted pain will put a self-aware edge on you that will appeal to many. After all, mixing self-loathing with love may not produce the smoothest relationships, but it usually guarantees the most memorable.

FISHING FOR LOVE

While a slut, as Janis Joplin put it, is "like a turtle hiding beneath its horny shell," a self-loather looking for love is like a turtle pried out from beneath its horny shell and dangled over a soup pot.

When you're looking for love, many self-appointed advice-givers will be quick to exploit your vulnerability in order to sell you books. But beware: many of their recommendations are designed for self-loathing-impaired persons. Just check our bookshelf and see for yourself . . .

FROM OUR BOOKSHELF . . . THE BOOK: "MARS AND VENUS ON A DATE"

Author: John Gray

The Advice: "Finding the right person for you is like hitting the center of the target in archery."

What a self-loathing-impaired person makes of this advice: "Ready, aim, fire!"

What a self-loather makes of this advice: "Hmmm. What Gray seems to be suggesting is that if my current Someone is too mean, I should correct my aim and try dating somebody nicer. If that nicer person is too dull, try dating somebody who's nice but more interesting. If that nice, interesting person is too ugly, try dating somebody nice, interesting, and achingly beautiful, and if that nice, interesting, maddeningly gorgeous person is too poor, try dating somebody who's kind, fascinating, ravishing, and a billionaire. When that person rejects me for someone nicer, more interesting, better-looking, wealthier, and higher born, I can try putting on heavy clothes, twisting a garland of rue around my head, and jumping into a swollen Danish stream."

Clearly, John Gray's advice won't do for a self-loathing romantic like you. Even more than a mate who meets a set of escalating criteria (as Gray advises), you'll need someone who can appreciate your talent for bashing yourself over the head. Sadly, there is no methodical way to find people you enjoy self-loathing with. You just have to keep seeking at random—and hating yourself for failing—until you find one.

YOUR QUESTIONS ANSWERED

A shy student with bold, beautiful shoulders: Hi. I'm a self-loather, and I think I've met someone I'm interested in.

SL4B: Congratulations.

Shy: Thanks. You, um . . . you probably get asked this all the time, but, is it better for me to reek of self-loathing on a first date, or should I let the other person gradually discover it as she gets to know me better?

SL4B: Ah. You began, "You probably get asked this all the time." Care to explain that opening?

Shy: Um, "Don't hate me for asking a boring, ordinary question . . . ?"

SL4B: . . . as much as you hate yourself for it?

Shy: Yeah, sure.

SL4B: Aren't you also asking me to admire you for knowing that you are boring more than I hate you for being boring?

Shy: Well, self-awareness, like you said, should count for something.

SL4B: It's true; I did say that. But you weren't self-aware about how much information about yourself you were offering me, were you?

Shy: You're saying I'm too much of a beginner to be able to control how much self-loathing I reveal.

SL4B (nods): As a beginner, unsure of how your self-loathing will be received, yes, the danger is that you will reveal it accidentally—and clumsily—rather than charmingly. Here are some sample "dos" and don'ts" for exhibiting the tip of your vice to a potential mate:

 **Tip**

Please note, beginners . . . when and how to reveal your self-loathing is not an issue for professional self-loathers because they are already famous for loathing themselves.

COURTSHIP DOS AND DON'TS FOR SELF-LOATHERS

Situation: Your date asks you about your family.

DO: Describe family's selling points and virtues. Mom used to win beauty contests; Dad won a Purple Heart; great-grandparents bravely emigrated to escape persecution, etc. But hint that this isn't the whole story.

DON'T: Spill. Save the divorces, the domestic violence, and the tribal vendettas for the third date.

Situation: After accepting date's recreational drug, become violently ill on date's carpet.

DO: Once you recover say, "That hasn't happened to me since that evening I threw up on _____." (Insert the name of Snoop Dogg, Al Gore III, Quentin Crisp, or Ambassador to France.)

DON'T: Attempt to say "Sorry!" between heaves.

Situation: Your date keeps talking about bands you've never heard of, making you feel completely clueless.

DO: Say, "I wrote a song once," then sing something tuneless and childlike about knowing somebody who knows the name of every band in the world.

DON'T: Pretend you know things you don't; announce at the end of date's monologue, "You know, I didn't understand a word of what you just said"; or, if you are a male, say, "You're smarter than I am," as if anyone cares.

Situation: Your date remarks that your résumé sounds a bit spotty.

DO: Look earnestly at date and say, "Look: Loathing me is a full-time job; it's hard and dangerous and it wears a person down. But it's my job, not yours. So as long as we're together, I don't want you to get mixed up in it."

DON'T: Cry. At least not on the outside.

GETTING HOOKED ON LOVE

Nervous woman in excessively ruffled designer blouse that's never going to make it through the dry cleaners: People keep saying it's impossible to love others if you hate yourself but I do it all the time.

SL4B: And the question is?

Blouse: Am I so weird?

SL4B: Well, let's see: if by "love" you mean an exchange of affection, empathy, and erotic connection, then it would be very weird if an utter self-loather managed it, although it's less of a problem for partials. But, if by "love" you mean possessiveness? Fixation? Bodice heaving? That kind of love mixes well with massive self-loathing. Also with lots of ruffles.

So the short answer is yes—self-loathers can love as deeply and strongly as anyone else: just don't expect many simple pleasures from the experience.

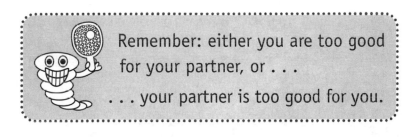

Remember: either you are too good for your partner, or . . .
. . . your partner is too good for you.

No-nonsense man from small investment firm: Is there any particular style you can recommend for a self-loather in love?

SL4B: Your best bet is plain old vanilla self-loathing— in which you just generally can't bear yourself and look to a partner to come up with a version of you that you can stand, then dismiss their opinion as biased. Your partner will enjoy your frequent demands for reassurance, your wounded cries of "How could you?" and your plaintive pillow talk—including, "God, I hate myself!"; "You're so much better than I am"; and, "Am I the best you've ever had? Seriously?"

Romance Tip: Don't assume that your partner loathes the same things about yourself that you do. Your partner might let you get away with things you thought were repulsive—and point out new flaws you didn't know you had!

YOUR QUESTIONS ANSWERED

Q: Should I get romantically involved with another self-loather, or would that be more fun than I deserve?

A: Go ahead—but try to find someone who has a complementary set. For example, someone who hates themselves for having trusted Tom Cruise while you hate yourself for trashing your head on blow. It worked for Nicole Kidman and her Aussie, Keith Urban.

Q: The more wonderful my lover seems to me the more repulsive I feel I am. But if I choose anyone less wonderful, I'll feel stupid for settling short. Which form of self-loathing is best for me?

 A: You don't have to choose, yo. Ping-ponging from abjection to entitlement until it is too late to have children is a perfectly good option!

Q: If I manage "to love and be loved in return" like it says in that song from Moulin Rouge, *won't I be too damn happy to self-loathe, or is there some way to do both?*

A: You saw the movie. When you find true love and experience happiness, the other person will sell out and die, and then you can hate yourself for not having known how to save her (or him).

Q: When my lover cheats on me, I'm the one who does all the self-loathing afterwards. What's with that?

A: Obviously, you're inadequate. It's your job to be so desirable that no one will want anyone else, ever.

Q: What if I'm fabulous and my lover cheats anyway?

A: How come you didn't notice from the start that you were dealing with an emotional cripple? (You must be a rotten judge of character.) Or, you knew they'd cheat, but fell in love with them anyway. (You're so self-defeating!) The good news is, whatever went wrong, you were in control of it!

 **Tip**

Advanced self-loathers may take famous lovers. Agree for years that you are less important than they. Then leave and try to worship yourself the way you once worshipped them. Fail. Instead, collect uplifting thoughts. (See Boyd Inspiration Box, page 130.)

INSPIRATION !

Quickie

When Christie Brinkley got publicly humiliated by her husband's affair with a teen in a toy store, she took on more self-loathing than she wanted. But the ex-supermodel, having divorced three times before, had learned to handle surplus suffering deftly. She quickly converted all her excess shame into disgust for her mate, divorced him—and started dating Paul McCartney. Beginners can only dream of such swift switchbacks!

CUTTING BAIT

Q: How do I know when it's time to hate myself for leaving a relationship rather than for staying in it?

A: Under the following circumstances, that spasm of self-loathing means . . .

TIME TO FIND SOMEONE NEW

1. When the sweet, vulnerable person you're dumping for a hotter one starts to cry and you feel like such a worm you consider staying;

2. When you realize this is exactly the sort of lunatic you vowed never to see again, but obviously did;

3. When your lover or spouse can't stop looking at someone else;

4. When your lover or spouse keeps dancing with someone else;

5. When your lover or spouse goes home with someone else.

Master of Self-Loathing in Love: Johann Wolfgang von Goethe (1749–1832)

Goethe's first big success, *Die Leiden des jungen Werthers* (see quote, Part I), was said to have inspired more than 2,000 suicides because people reading it suddenly felt that an unfulfilled love made their lives worthless. But, in translation, *The Sorrows of Young Werther* inspired Mary Shelley to create Dr. Frankenstein's lovesick monster, whose sufferings have made millions of self-loathers feel more alive.

ONE LAST QUESTION FROM THE FLOOR

Cute, gloomy teen: If I say "I love you," and the other person doesn't say it back, should I loathe myself or just jump off a bridge?

SL4B: You're young yet. I'd say go with the loathing, for now.

THIS CHAPTER'S MANTRA

Love makes the world
go 'round and 'round
until I fall
on my ass.

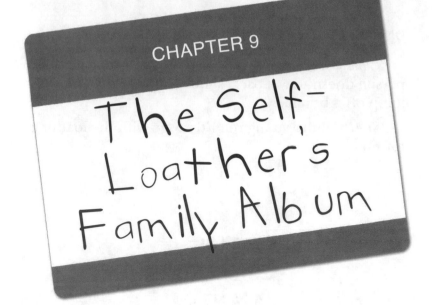

CHAPTER 9

The Self-Loather's Family Album

"I've been a problem baby, a lousy son, a distant brother, an off-putting neighbor, a piss-poor student, a worrisome seatmate, an unreliable employee, a bewildering lover, a frustrating confidant, and a crappy husband. Among the things I do pretty well at this point I'd have to list darts, re-closing Stay-Fresh boxes, and staying out of the way."

"The Gun Lobby," Jim Shepard

JUST BECAUSE the way you feel about yourself is your fault, doesn't mean that your relations can't augment your self-loathing. Simply let them know where you're vulnerable, and let love do the rest.

Because family life is the cradle and grave of self-rejection, the topic is too huge to cover here. So what we'll do is trace the origins of self-loathing in childhood (skirting most of the molestations and abductions so well-described in bestsellers), then skip and skim our way through adulthood.

THE SELF-LOATHING OF MINORS

Because you owe your parents your life, it is easy to hold a grudge against them and even easier to detest yourself for your ingratitude. Try it and see. You can loathe them whether they chain you up in the basement or merely don't understand that music didn't end with "Chain of Fools." Although many facets of childhood self-hatred are no longer suitable for adults, they can still inspire new twists in your mature style. So let's take a rapid tour up the developmental timeline of self-loathing with that in mind.

NEWBORNS

As far as we know, a newborn's self-loathing is elusive because at times it has no self to hate whereas at other times it self encompasses everything around it or coming out of it, so any disgust it experiences is self-loathing.

INFANTS

In 1949, the French psychologist Jacques Lacan theorized that a modern infant's self-loathing begins between six and eighteen months, when it first recognizes itself in a mirror. The infant promptly feels that the jumble of legs, gurgles, fingers, and giddiness it experiences as its self are inferior to the visual "ego ideal" in the glass, so it forms a lifelong ambition to be what it isn't—a tidy, if oversimplified image of a person: In other words, a celebrity.

As an infant develops, it discovers that it has rivals. Its mother may refuse to pick it up, pet or feed it because she has better things to do, and one of those better things is to sleep with other people. The infant then faces a choice about whether to:

(a) loathe itself for being unlovable;

(b) loathe itself for wanting to kill its rivals;

(c) start to feel like loathing its mother but then get scared of frightening her off and starving, so turning its fury on its helpless little self in a twisty way, warping it for life; or

(d) looking upon all of life as one great surprise and delight, postponing self-loathing until it is old enough to read.

(Which of these options did YOU choose?)

TOTS

When you are a child, your self-loathing is encouraged in several ways. Here are three that tend to stick with you:

1. First, giants are constantly telling you that whatever you want to eat, touch, jump upon, or pull to the floor will end in tears. Do it anyway and the giants speak harshly to you until you cry. So you get to choose whether to hate yourself for being curious or disobedient, or both.

2. Second, grown-ups find you funniest when you'd like most to be taken seriously. In short: dignity is not, for you, a ride you're tall enough to get on.

3. Third, as you grow older, you develop contempt for your own babyhood, "I am NOT a baby!" until the next baby becomes "the baby" and you have to regress to get attention. And once you do, they notice your desperate ploy and laugh at you. The lesson here—that you can't win—is a valuable one.

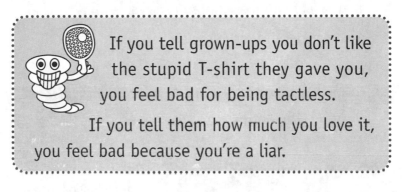

If you tell grown-ups you don't like the stupid T-shirt they gave you, you feel bad for being tactless.

If you tell them how much you love it, you feel bad because you're a liar.

TWEENS

As a tween, you begin to invent ways to handle self-loathing, but you are still dependent on your family to inflame your self consciousness and shame. They can do this simply by trying to help you. Frank talks, gifts of condoms, or talk of eternal damnation all work equally well. But if you are a tween whose parents do not volunteer to mortify you, there are ways of getting them to cooperate.

For example, start hating your body parts (as instructed in Part I, Chapter 3), but flaunt them anyway.

Your family, afflicted with forbidden desires, will be confused by your flaunted body parts. They will either deny that your body is repulsive (because they are liars), or they will agree that your body is less than wonderful (because they are jealous saboteurs). Thus, you will learn to combine self-loathing with mistrust.

In any case, your family's emotionally complicated reaction to the stage you're in will make you hate them for no clear (to you) reason, and that will make you feel so fabulously evil and guilty you'll be inspired to devise even more fantastic and alarming outfits, a talent that can serve you well if you go into fashion, music, or psychic advising.

TEENS

The five most frequently asked questions are:

1. Why do I hate myself and hate my parents even more?

Answer: Hormones.

2. Why do I hate my family for not understanding how sexy and touching and beautiful my hating myself is?

Answer: Hormones.

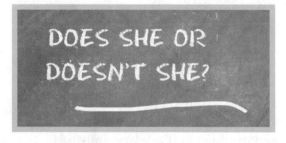

After spending her childhood in Disney's wholesome media factory, Lindsay Lohan broke out to star in Tina Fey's hit film, *Mean Girls*, and started getting adult roles. But on the cusp of a successful film and singing career, Lohan balked. Within a year's time, her frolics included crashing cars, DUIs, and getting caught carrying her own cocaine (instead of having someone else carry it for her). So she's sabotaging her career, but does she loathe herself? Her music video, "Confessions of a Broken Heart (Daughter to Father)," begged us to care about her problems with her dad. But all anyone really cares about is that Lohan appear on set on time. Her attitude seems to have changed to: "If you don't really care about me, I won't either." That suggests her problem is adolescent self-pity rather than self-loathing. Either way, she will want to swat herself on the nose with a rolled-up copy of *Variety* once she sobers up. Verdict? Roughly 50% self-loather and 50% brat.

3. *Why do I keep feeling that millions of people are better at life than I am, and that those who aren't do not deserve to live?*

Answer: Hormones.

4. *Why do I care so much more about who's dating whom than about actually, like, doing more about climate change than my parents, who are all blah blah blah about it but have huge carbon footprints?*

Answer: Hormones.

5. *What's wrong with my saying "whatever" and "like" and "rilly" and "phat" and "bee-atch" or something equally, like, bangin' every two seconds?*

Answer: What isn't?

SIBLINGS

Many aspiring self-loathers torture their siblings in the hope of feeling lower than dirt about it later. But it turns out that putting chicken livers in your siblings' shoes or burning their novels in the backyard barbeque produce little remorse at the time and only a shiver of guilt once you have grown up. In fact, reminiscing about the torture of siblings produces (in most cases) only nostalgia and merriment all around. If your goal is to experience mid-life regret, the best bet is to squander your best years agonizing about your own shortcomings instead of creating amusing memories of putting silly putty in siblings' beds, or bursting in upon them dressed as a Martian while they are attempting to lose their virginity.

Warning: If you have no sibling to torture, do not try to substitute a pet, classmate, or family servant. True, you will loathe yourself if you do torture any of them, but you will be punished so severely that you will end up seeing yourself as a mere victim rather than as a nasty little punk. The demotion will take all the mirth and grandeur out of your self-loathing, and we don't want that.

SELF-LOATHING QUALITY TIME FOR ADULTS

GROWN CHILDREN

Apart from disappointing yourself, disappointing your parents is one of the most universal excuses for feeling like a soiled diaper. It's also surprisingly easy to do.

Double your feelings of inadequacy! Get your family to flog you with these casual phrases:

1. "All we want is for you to be happy."

2. "You were always such a (adjective) child" (meaning either that you have not matured or that you have degenerated horribly).

3. "It would make (name of relative) so (happy/proud) if you would _____!
   (Insert one or more of the following options)
   —Go (back) to med school

   —Marry the person you're dating

   —Marry a friend whose sexual orientation doesn't match yours

   —Have babies with either of two preceding or with someone you're considering divorcing

   —Have babies with somebody rich and well-connected

   —Have babies

   —Lose a little weight (meaning a lot)

   —Wear your hair so that your cheeks look like water balloons

   —Dress like the dullards, snobs, and dweebs you despise

—Do something far more prestigious than anything you are doing now

—Give your mother (or any other relative) a big hug

—Visit more often

—Give big hug, visit more often, and change bedpan

(If Jewish, have relative add: "Is that too much to ask?")

Q: What's the fastest way to get a year's worth of self-loathing from my family in one fell swoop?

A: Christmas (Chanukah, Kwanzaa).

Q: How can I empower my family to feed my self-loathing regularly so that I don't have to wait for Christmas?

A: E-mail.

Q: Should I ask my family and friends to encourage my feeling worthless?

A: Scientific research suggests that they will help you more if they do the opposite. According to studies at the psychology department of Ohio State University released in June of 1999, people who doubt themselves a lot have different thinking patterns from those who don't, and spending hours trying to list their good points only makes them feel worse! So when you really want to hate yourself, tell your well-wishers to build you up by listing your pathetically few and inconsequential virtues and accomplishments.

PARENTS

The self-loathing parent has two goals: One, to raise children who self-loathe adorably—either in a self-deprecating way that will allow the child to rise in, say, the cultural studies department of a Midwestern university, or else in a wrath-of-Khan way that will make people tremble at the sound of your family name, whether whispered in a mob restaurant or shouted out at a celebrity roast.

The second major goal of self-loathing parents is to blame themselves for things over which they have little control.

To achieve these goals, first and foremost, use your ping-pong paddle.

 In putting your child to sleep, for example, you can follow child-rearing expert, Dr. Richard Ferber, and let the child cry itself blue. The theory is that it will soon learn to put itself to sleep and everybody will be better-rested for each new day's self-loathing.

 Another school of child-rearing tells you to pick the child up when it cries and comfort it until it is one and a half, no matter what. That theory holds that children need love and security to feel confident enough to explore their self-loathing bravely and inquisitively.

 A third school—your great-grandmother's or her nanny's—tells you that the baby is probably teething and a rag soaked in a sedative should quiet it down. That theory is that life is painful for self-loathers, and that opiates do help, at least if sucked through a clean rag in moderate doses.

Since each one of these schools thinks the others are wrong, you need only start believing one while doing another to rev your parental self-loathing up to tournament speed.

How this all affects your child will be revealed in time. There's just no way of knowing how a speechless, mushy little brain is interpreting the cry-yourself-blue, suck-on-this, or I-am-your-servant method. Is it the path to autonomy, or the first chapter in a *Mommy Dearest* memoir? While you are waiting to find out, you are free to imagine the worst and accuse yourself for having foisted it on your unfortunate offspring.

"Spoiling" children is, overall, the best source of self-loathing for parent and child both. Some children, given every material comfort, once fully grown trot off to Nepal to prostrate themselves at the hem of a monk, or else they give in to the "spoiled" identity completely, wandering through dilapidated mansions while singing the score of *Grey Gardens*. Still others shame indulgent families by becoming oil tycoons, presidents, and pre-emptive warmongers.

But if you think that indulging your child is the only way to get spectacular results, think again. You can teach your child "the value of a dollar" by making it work for every cent—with the same exact result.

The point? Again: all you can do in the early years is to anticipate the worst and flagellate yourself in advance for causing it.

YOUR QUESTIONS ANSWERED

Q: Will it harm my children if I brood about my bad parenting?

A: Studies show that an effective way to harm your children is to misunderstand them or ignore what they're feeling, so if you brood about your inadequacies hard and often enough, yes, it will distract you from their reaction to the latest school shooting and they will go mad. But if the experts are right, you would do best to brood about your *children's* inadequacies, especially as defined by them.

Q: Should I tell my kids that they're smart, or let them figure out that they're stupid for themselves?

A: Well, a Columbia University survey has found that indiscriminate praise turns students into praise junkies, incapable of persistence and hard work. So if you want your kids to be the kind of self-loathers who have high self-esteem yet no real accomplishments, tell them how

Every Girl's Fantasy

Wonderful Today, Pattie Boyd's "auto-biography" (written "with" Penny Junor), teaches you how to loathe yourself for marrying two rock 'n roll demigods and inspiring several rock classics! Her life with Beatle George Harrison was degrading: he swapped her out for another rocker's wife, and later, when he found out she was sleeping with Cream's Eric Clapton, proposed another swap. Clapton wrote "Layla" about how much he wanted her, but after they married, his addictions and acts of abuse (battery, rape) along with her infertility and wine-guzzling did them in. (Clapton wrote "The Shape You're In," about Boyd, once the thrill was gone.) Living alone, Boyd claims to have achieved independent self-regard, but although she is no longer an ego-battered love doll for brilliant troubadours, her emotional autonomy is a bit iffy. Her tell-all book may not be bitter, but she hadn't intended to write one until Clapton announced his plans to publish his. Because she did, though, we can thank self-loathing once again for making life more interesting.

smart they are every day, and be careful not to praise their good work habits, should any accidentally show up.

Q: Do you think Robin Williams loathes himself?

A: Glad you completely changed the topic. Demonstrating that you are more interested in celebrities than in your kids is a lesson they can't learn soon enough—or ever forget.

SELF-LOATHING AND MARRIAGE

Single beginners often ask whether marriage will impair their self-loathing, and the answer is an unequivocal "Yes and no." So many opportunities for marital self-blame now occur outside of marriage that many wonder why any gay or lesbian self-loathers would be eager to tie the knot. The answer is that there are a few special perks the married self-loather can enjoy, and homosexuals and other co-habitants rightly feel they should be allowed to enjoy them.

These are:

1. Waking up and realizing that you married someone of the wrong sex;

2. Understanding that your miserable marriage was made holy by God and leaving it is going to send you to Hell for all eternity (aka "the contract marriage perk");

3. Realizing that all marriages have their ups and downs but you're too much of an impatient baby to make it through the downs, and besides: it isn't all THAT sacred an institution;

4. Waking up and realizing that your divorce will cost you a fucking fortune because you were too jelly-headed to get a prenup;

5. Getting asked for a divorce by somebody you thought loved you, or could, at minimum, stick with you while sleeping with everyone else in town, but who is willing to pay a fucking fortune to get rid of you and who you were dumb enough to marry, even though all your friends warned you it would never work out.

Q: What role does snoring, tossing, tooth grinding, sleep-walking, and wheezing play in a self-loather's marriage?

A: A sleep study underway at the Sleep Disorders Center at Rush University Medical Center showed that a husband's snoring increased both partners' daytime fatigue and nearly halved the wife's marital satisfaction. "This is not a mild problem," concluded Rosalind Cartwright, Ph.D., the Center's founder. Trapped in a dark room with a raucous sleeper, spouses who think of themselves as "nice," "decent," and "loving" can suddenly horrify themselves by experiencing the murderous impulses of a baby-eating dingo. The best thing, in such cases, is to squirt the snoring mate with a plant mister, or drop a piece of cat food into mate's gaping maw, or scorch mate lightly with a flamethrower and watch with satisfaction as mate splutters or gags before quieting down. Be extra nice in the a.m., and if your unwitting mate asks, "Why are you being so good to me?" you can feel deliciously (if only partially) loathsome when you say, "Because I love you so much."

ONE LAST QUESTION

Q: How can I turn my loathing for my spouse into self-loathing?

A: If you believe that holy matrimony makes a couple "one person," you already have.

Masters of Family Self-Loathing: Robert Crumb (1943–) and Aline Kominsky-Crumb (1948–)

Since the late '60s and early '70s, Robert Crumb and Aline Kominsky-Crumb have made cartoons about their shameless peculiarities. Their long-open marriage, based on a shared appreciation of his big-leg fetish and let-me-ride-you-like-a-pony predilection, is a model of how to make spousal weirdness cheery. *Self-Loathing Comics*, drawn half by him, half by her, should inspire any of you self-loathers trying to build a stable relationship from a hatred of your nose, ethnicity, sexuality, dependencies, infidelities, and materialism—and to show you how to build it in Provence with someone funny you (mostly) love.

THIS
CHAPTER'S
MANTRA

Home is where I hang
myself.

CHAPTER 10

Workplace Self-Loathing

"She changed when she got the new job. She was always intense, but, before, the intensity had somewhere to go: she could worry about tenants' rights, and slum landlords, and kids living in places without running water. Now she's just intense about work—how much she has, the pressure she's under, how she's doing, what the partners think of her, that kind of stuff. And when she's not being intense about work, she's being intense about why she shouldn't be intense about work, or this kind of work, anyway."

—*High Fidelity* (1995), Nick Hornby

YOU CAN LOATHE yourself for having only $10 or for having only $10 billion. You can kick yourself for spending the rent money on shoes or for purchasing a house before you do a termite test. But of all the ways money can enlarge your self-loathing quotient, few are as deliciously shame-ridden as earning it.

Whatever you do, whatever you make, the more you invest your self-worth in your salary and career standing, the better your return in self-loathing can be. Ambition, competition, initiative—all the things that the work world rewards in cash it will match in self-loathing if you are not afraid to let it.

BUCKLING DOWN

Because these days no job lasts a lifetime, *Self-Loathing for Beginners* will focus on portable self-loathing skills.

THE SEVEN HABITS OF SUCCESSFUL WORKPLACE SELF-LOATHERS

Don't wait for Donald Trump to tell you you're fired to feel like a loser. Careful attention to detail will uncover hundreds of opportunities to belittle yourself on your employer's time!

1. Pay attention! Let no germ of disrespect escape your notice, no matter how tiny. Was a great idea of yours ignored? Not invited to lunch? Asked to train your replacement? Great self-loathers soak up disrespect wherever they find it and take it to heart.
2. Savor the horror. Self-loathers are often told "Don't sweat the small stuff (and it's all small stuff)." Then we are told, "God is in the details." Don't let baffling, lose-lose instructions like this slip by you: stop and smell the small stuff.

3. Blur, blur, blur. Smudge those distracting lines between job performance and personal worth. Your self-loathing will run much more smoothly without them.

4. Learn from your mistakes. Anything you can screw up once, you can screw up again, and better!

5. Be creative! Dare to harangue yourself for things no one has ever harangued themselves for before. For example: Failed to smile warmly at the receptionist? "So self-defeating of me, to alienate the gatekeeper." Or, loathe yourself for smiling at her too warmly—"Fool: You could get sacked for sexual harassment!" You've got an imagination. Use it.

6. Don't be afraid to give your best ideas away. You'll always have more ideas that people can steal as they pass you on their way up.

7. Dare to fail and fail again—and again! Every successful person knows that you can't succeed if you don't risk failure. But self-loathers, heads up: you can't successfully fail if you don't risk failure either.

BONUS ATTRIBUTION– CONTESTED QUOTE

"Success is going from failure to failure without losing your enthusiasm."

"Success is going from failure to failure without loss of enthusiasm."

"Courage is going from failure to failure without losing your enthusiasm."

—*All three attributed online to Winston Churchill (the first also attributed to Abraham Lincoln).*

A SELF-LOATHER'S ALBUM OF WORK SONGS

All over the world, work songs help chain gangs bear the tedium and pain of hard labor. Here are some songs to help beginners endure their difficult but civilization-building self-loathing:

HORIZONTAL MOTION

THE SELF-LOATHER'S PORTABLE TRAVEL GUIDE

To the Tune of . . .	Sing
"Take This Job and Shove It"	Take This Job and Shove Me
"Strawberry Fields Forever"	Steal My Ideas, You Bastard
"Come On, Baby, Light My Fire"	Will This E-mail Get Me Fired?
"Where Is the Love?"	Where Is My Lunch?
"Fuck That (I'm a Ho)"	Fuck That (I'm a Hack)
"Unchain My Heart"	Return My Stapler
"Sex Machine"	Snack Machine
"She Works Hard for the Money"	We Work Hard for a Monkey
"Bad Company"	Bad Company

As you move from company to company, take with you these seven abnormally short self-loathing ideas.

1. Fido—Whether you work as a meatpacker or a corporate consultant, some boss, government agency, client, or customer treats you like a stray. And makes you heel.

2. Widget—Ask yourself: "Does the world really need another _____?" (Fill in whatever you are producing: lawsuit, business suit, hovel, novel, Baywatch, baby.) Yours is a worthless endeavor.

3. You work for Skittles—For shame. You have sold your liberty for a worthless endeavor.

4. Trash—Visualize how disposable you are when you are (a) overworked (picture a slave building an Egyptian pyramid) or (b) under-challenged (imagine an old tire lying by the roadside).

5. Hamster Wheel—Outdoors, indoors, wrong floor, bad view, too small, toxic furniture and lighting. Your workspace is a cage; so what does that make you?

6. Dopey—You have co-workers you wouldn't even wish on . . . on yourself! You must have been awfully snotty to Gandhi in a former life to be stuck in a cubicle farm with such clueless dweebs.

7. Happy—Positive attitude police are on your case. What they say is, "Lighten up," but what they really mean is, "Enjoy yourself, you morose little turd, or I'm the mower and your ass is grass." Why can't you be one of the sunny people?

If you stay late at work (take work home, work on a holiday), scold yourself for being a workaholic.

If you stick to nine-to-five, face it: you're not a team player (competitive enough to succeed).

VERTICAL PROMOTION

THE SELF-LOATHER'S SHORTLIST . . .

. . . of things you can loathe yourself for either enduring OR perpetrating: Random drug testing, sexual harassment, discrimination, poorly maintained restrooms, lack of flex time, doubled workload, benefits cut, wages frozen, pensions cancelled, subordinates belittled, backstabbing, bootlicking, glad-handing, sucking up, ratting out, buckpassing, credit-grabbing, jargon-spouting, hypocritical speechifying, kicking someone in the shin, or getting kicked upstairs. (Congratulations!)

> **BONUS CAREER-PLANNING QUOTE**
>
> "Because right now, this is a job. If I advance any higher, this would be my career. And if this were my career, I'd have to throw myself in front of a train."—*Jim Halpert (PB John Krasinski)*, The Office, *"Health Care"* episode, by Paul Lieberstein

FAILURE

QUESTIONS FROM THE FLOOR

Nervous woman in excessively ruffled designer blouse that's never going to make it through the dry cleaners: I just got laid off and I'm loathing myself so heavily that I'm having trouble doing it with the kind of panache you're calling for. I'm in the middle of a conversation with the dry cleaner and I just break down and start blubbering. And then I loathe myself even more. Then I tell myself to buck up and stop feeling so sorry for myself, that God or the Great Spirit or whatever is out there either loves me or doesn't care, but it doesn't help. Any suggestions?

SL4B: Aw, gee. When you're a natural-born self-loather the self-abuse that follows involuntary job loss can be a little too much of a good thing, I know.

Permanent Vacation? Why the Hell Not?

Alice James, sister to brilliant intellectuals William and Henry, took to her bed with "ailments" (as did numerous other well-off 19th-century women too smart for their traditionally constricted roles), and never left.

To dampen excessive pain, many sensitive self-loathers will amp up the agony in other facets of their lives. Whiskey, malingering, humiliating yourself in front of the dry cleaner (as you've done), speedballs, irascibility towards loved ones (until they leave you), and even a fender bender or two can overload your circuits until they short out, landing you in some Betty Ford-like rehab facility from which you will most likely emerge ready to accept that the torment of self-loathing isn't quite as bad as the searing pain you get when you try to avoid the torment of self-loathing. It's not an elegant solution, but it has been known to work.

After their second firing, advanced self-loathers tend to "go to ground," retreating to their rooms for months like teen practitioners of hikikomori in Japan.

Warning: Going to ground requires a competent support staff—long-suffering parents, famous brothers, or paid servants.

A professional self-loather finds a stylish and self-serving way to handle the agony of disgrace. Currently most popular: serving a short jail term (Lil' Kim, for perjury), starting a new perfume line (Paris Hilton's is called "Paris Hilton" instead of "DUI"), or forming a production company (will rapper Ja Rule's so-far-obscure Focus

Vision Inc. take the focus away from his latest arrest for gun possession?). When demoted, Presidents Jimmy Carter and Bill Clinton side-dished their disgrace and made philanthropy the day's special. So did billionaire media czar Ted Turner, once he lost his media empire to Time Warner. Not so Britney Spears, who seems to be using disgrace as a way of trashing her product line. (See "Does She or Doesn't She?" this page.)

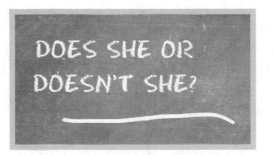

Anybody home? Although Britney Spears seems a shoo-in for most self-loathing pop-tart, her head-shaving, crotch-flashing, and rehab-escaping seem safe compared to Lohan's car-crash-on-freeway habit. (Spears restricts her fender-bending to parking lots.) Can it be that Spears isn't attacking herself so much as her brand? She was fine as long as she was telling millions of fans that she was a virgin while sleeping with 'N Sync's Justin Timberlake. The virgin was the marketing whore—the multimillion-dollar spin-off industry—and the woman having sex was her. But after Timberlake gave her game away, the line blurred. There's plenty to loathe about her life: She's not enjoying motherhood; she lost the right guy once and married the wrong guy twice; she's so valuable a commodity that no one, including her, can imagine how becoming less of one could be a step up. But even if she hates her life, it's not clear she thinks it's something she owns. When she blew off her "comeback" at the Video Music Awards, she seemed like she was taking a potshot at her career the way teens knock over mailboxes, as a vandal, not as someone violating something close to their heart. Verdict? She got tired of being a Slave 4 U.

No-nonsense man from small investment firm: Is it true that corporations are learning to self-loathe, too?

SL4B: At last! Better yet, despite their legal status as persons, corporations cannot actually speak or write. So opportunities for bloggers who can translate a company's mea culpas into seductive confessions are multiplying faster than . . . (Get some blogging practice by finishing this humorous comparison for me, and put it on your résumé.)

Bicoastal metrosexual in retail promotions: May I count bungling my personal finances as a job if I do it full-time?

SL4B: Great idea. And you can be your own bullying boss when you do it! Chew yourself out with these pre-fab put-downs.

PERFORMANCE CRITIQUE FOR THE SELF-EMPLOYED SELF-LOATHER

Hey, Shit-for-brains, why the hell can't you . . .

. . . stick to a budget—whatever that is?

. . . stop wasting money on (whatever necessities you waste money on)?

. . . get organized?—As if.

. . . start a billion-dollar business, like Mary Kay or Google . . .

. . . the way (insert name of dork you hated in high school) did?

. . . cut yourself some slack?—Oh, I forgot: you don't know how.

Adorable schlub from either Ohio, Brooklyn, or both: Is it better for me to take my self-loathing out on subordinates or to let it secretly eat me alive?

SL4B: You are a true beginner! Obviously the first option is a symptom of the second. And vice versa.

Woman with scary eyebrows and red nails: How do busy, famous, successful people manage to find time to self-loathe?

SL4B: Excellent question, to which there's no single answer. Here are three:

PROFESSIONAL SELF-LOATHING TIME SAVERS

1. Talk show host Larry King—wears suspenders to produce wedgies that make him feel slightly raped all day.

2: Britain's ex-prime minister, Tony Blair—so as not to waste valuable time during his country's war with Iraq, figured out how to loathe himself in his sleep!

3. *Seinfeld's* Michael Richards (Cosmo Kramer on the TV series)—when his career slid, packed so much self-loathing into the tiniest part of his mind, that it burst out of him in a self-destructive racist tirade—much like a beginner.

BONUS FAILURE-MANAGEMENT QUOTE

"Whatever else we are intended to do, we are not intended to succeed; failure is the fate allotted. . . . Our business is to continue to fail in good spirits."—*Robert Louis Stevenson's diary*

Cynical dude in old T-shirt: Do I have to be kind to friends less successful than I?

SL4B: If you can find any, yes.

Cocky wiseass with stubble: How come all telemarketers don't hate themselves?

SL4B: They don't?

SQUIRMING AND WRITHING—
THREE WORKPLACE EXERCISES

If you're too busy to work out, keep yourself fit by aerobicizing your self-loathing.

1. Think of the one thing you would never do for a million dollars and contemplate doing it for 20 dollars. (Repeat set 3X)

2. Spend an afternoon at your workplace writing out all the great things you could be doing with your life, but aren't. To let go of your regrets, tear up the paper and toss into the air. Crawl around picking up the pieces, one by one. Put them back together. Toss and throw until you feel the burn.

3. Hyperventilate.

ONE LAST QUESTION

Balding intellectual: As a beginner, how can the two little words "intellectual prostitution" help me despise my job and myself for doing it?

SL4B: If you came up with that question yourself, you are no longer a beginner.

Master of Workplace Self-Loathing: Frederick Winslow Taylor (1856–1915)

One reason that workplaces are factories of self-loathing is "scientific management." The visionary self-loather Frederick Taylor started breaking down industrial jobs into small increments and timing each to find "the one best way" to do everything. His time-motion studies let employers replace workers' artisanal skills with robot-like routines in jobs of every description. Despite later efforts to re-humanize the dot-com workplace, Taylorism itself was computerized and automated. It now micromanages everyone from video-game coders to burger flippers.

THIS CHAPTER'S MANTRA

Yeah, but what
have I done lately?

CHAPTER 11

The Social Self-Loather

"Sunday was lethargic from the beginning as I wallowed in a morass of general and specific dislike and pity for most people, but me especially."

—Hillary Rodham in a letter postmarked Oct. 3, 1967.

AS DREW BARRYMORE reminded us early in 2007, "Life is high school," meaning, that society is generally gossipy, competitive, and cruel to anyone who cares what cute, cliquish people think of them. Anything others know about you is fair game: your looks, your look, your 'tude, your toys, your grades, your love life, your origins, you name it. In other words, life, like high school, will aggravate your self-doubt in thousands of ways—at once!

We'll sample a smattering of these opportunities in this chapter, along with various strategies of self-attack.

ACT LOCALLY

Everyday social life is a rich source of mortifying missteps and regrettable feelings. So many people have social anxieties and insecurities that when it comes to showing them off to advantage, you'll find stiff competition in any situation, from baby showers to pub crawls.

Out in public you always face a tricky choice—publicize the self-loathing, or suffer it in silence. As we will see, waving it around is sometimes a better approach than attempting (but failing) to hide it. The important thing to remember is not to try to rid yourself of social self-loathing entirely. That has been known to prove dangerous.

Warning: In the early '90s, 24-year-old Christopher McCandless, a well-off D.C. suburbanite, thought he could shed his self-loathing as the backwoodsman, "Alexander Supertramp." His 64-pound corpse was later found on Stampede Trail in Alaska. Although Sean Penn's movie, *Into the Wild*, imagines that when McCandless died of starvation his troubled spirit melted joyfully into the cosmos, all beginners who hope to lose themselves in nature are advised to pack instant noodles.

Here are the five key approaches to . . .

REVEALING SELF-LOATHING IN YOUR EVERYDAY SOCIAL LIFE

1. Announcing it—as did freelancer Lynn Darling once, to the Style editor of *The New York Times*: "I aim for a carefully calibrated equipoise between

overweening arrogance and abject self-hatred." If you are the taciturn type, you can wear the T-shirt emblazoned with Nirvana's song title, "I Hate Myself and I Want to Die."

2. Exuding it—via nervous self-consciousness, displaying ego-bruises (showing anger as you describe petty slights and wrongs), frantic clowning, desperation to please, false serenity, or ending every sentence with a rising intonation, as if you think so little of your ability to communicate (and the ability of others to understand) that you need constant reassurance that you're being understood.

3. Implying it—sucking up to others highlights your sense of inferiority; condescension implies a ladder of loathings in which the down-looker will suck up to someone on a higher rung.

4. Apologizing for existing—by apologizing a lot and then apologizing for so frequently apologizing.

5. Betraying it—with acts of *unconscious* self-loathing. Unconscious self-loathers are too preoccupied with all the other things going on around them to notice that their self-hatred is showing—until they get home and mentally replay their self-betrayals detail by detail.

If you've never (consciously) experienced unconscious self-loathing, here's . . .

A QUICK COURSE IN SELF-BETRAYAL

—At a party, display your fear of being dull by insisting that your date or mate tell certain amusing anecdotes when he or she is clearly not in the mood. "You know, the one where you throw up on the groom's mother . . . ?"

—Show that you feel inadequate as is by displaying a desperate need to be useful. For example, drag someone across the room to introduce them to someone else in a way that leaves both awkwardly speechless. "You both send me the funniest e-mails!"

—Tell a story suggesting that you are the most fabulous creature alive, then explain exactly how the story shows that, as if needing to convince yourself most of all. "See, before *I* did it, nobody thought to post a cat video on YouTube!"

—When asked what you have been working on, betray your terror of being exposed as a slacker by saying "Oh, projects," instead of the truth, which is "Nothing."

As you can see from the above list, quickly admitting to partial self-loathing lightens up a room, whereas leaking a concealed but pervasive self-loathing leaves people to guess wildly at how many of your hidden demons you hate, and that creates unnecessary discomfort. You might also try these . . .

FAVE SAVES

To charm others with your self-loathing, commit some of these minor social gaffes, then deliver the recovery line provided with a smile that says, "I'm making a little joke here, ha ha, because I am totally disgusted with myself":

Social gaffe: Arrive at a formal occasion in Hawaiian shorts, a minidress, or a hula skirt.

Recovery line: (*embarrassed gasp*) "Sorry about the outfit; I just came from a funeral."

Social gaffe: Bring the wrong gift, priced above or below what's appropriate and poorly matched to taste of recipient.

Recovery line: "Oh shit. You must have thousands of these."

Social gaffe: Botch a joke by leaving out a key line in the setup and attempting to re-insert it after the punch line, as in, "Oh, I forgot to say the part where a snake bit his penis!"

Recovery line (after an embarrassed pause): "Wanna hear another?"

Social gaffe: Forget your interlocutors' names and faces, ages of children, occasion of last encounter, topics covered, how you met.

Recovery line: "Sorry. I meant to forget everything I know about *me*."

Social gaffe: Quote someone who is standing in front of you, and quote them incorrectly.

Recovery line (after they correct you): "Oh yeah? Who's your source?"

Social gaffe: Try a few pratfalls, like tripping over an ottoman while drunk, knocking over a wineglass, or nearly losing your balance and flailing your arms wildly on the stairs to the opera's mezzanine.

Recovery line: "Did I tell you I studied ballet?"

Social gaffe: Making children cry when you smile at them.

Recovery line: "I think she likes me."

Social gaffe: Owning the leg someone's dog chooses to use as a sexual surrogate.

Recovery line: "I keep having these one-way relationships . . . I wish I could let him down easy without hurting his feelings."

Q: If everybody else in the room is betraying their self-loathing clumsily, won't it make them loathe themselves all the more if I'm charming and accepting of mine? And if they notice, won't that make them envious? And if they envy me, won't they turn on me? And won't I then feel dismal because I brought it down on myself?

A: Probably.

> **BONUS MANTRA**
>
> It doesn't take a village to self-loathe, but it helps.

ACT GLOBALLY

Once you have learned to self-loathe at a garden party to which you were not invited, taking social self-loathing up to the level of national or even global politics is not much of a stretch, even for beginners. Just use the following techniques and stylings.

THE LAW

Self-loathing isn't a crime (yet!), but many who get tired of punishing themselves often arrange to get the law to do the punishing for them. If you're considering this, be advised that incarceration seldom proves as relaxing as it looked in *Papillon* or *The Shawshank Redemption*. So, with a few exceptions in the music and financial sectors where prison terms have added to the allure of players like rap mogul 50 Cent and junk bond king, Michael Robert Milken, *SL4B* recommends that you start loathing yourself for your crimes before the police do.

Warning: Don't put off self-castigation like Enron CEO Ken Lay, who remained pleased with himself for bilking California of billions until well after he was caught.

Find Your Conventional Values Quotient

Will your self-loathing help you stay out of prison? If you committed the following crimes or misdeeds, how much would you and the public agree when it comes to judging your character?

Rate each sin or misdeed as follows:

1 = Awful, but funny   *4 = Proof of very, very bad character*
2 = Showed poor judgment   *5 = Downright evil.*
3 = Sign of bad character

Sin or Misdeed	(A) Conventional wisdom
Being rich. And silly. And drunk. And driving.	poor judgment 2
Killing an old lady because God is dead, and why not?	downright evil 5
Fixing a ballgame for money	bad 3
Losing a ballgame because you were up all night partying	poor judgment 2
Spending $7,800/yr. of employer's time, playing computer solitaire one hour a day at $25/hr.	poor judgment 2
Stealing employer's $800 jacket	very, very bad 4
Arranging an abortion for your daughter when you both think it's the same as murder	bad 3
Arranging for your lover to kill your spouse	downright evil 5
Sleeping with friend's betrothed in coatroom of friend's wedding	bad 3
Throwing up on groom's mother at friend's wedding	funny 1
TOTAL:	

Scoring: If your total in the last column is a negative number, your self-loathing helps you toe the line. If you score over 10, it won't keep you out of trouble, so find other uses for it.

(B) How guilty and bad I would feel (circle a number)	(A) minus (B) (negative numbers acceptable)
1 2 3 4 5	
1 2 3 4 5	
1 2 3 4 5	
1 2 3 4 5	
1 2 3 4 5	
1 2 3 4 5	
1 2 3 4 5	
1 2 3 4 5	
1 2 3 4 5	
1 2 3 4 5	

ENRICHING YOUR SELF-DOUBT WITH PARANOIA

Q: Sometimes I'm around people who, if I were them, would loathe me. And their loathing me would make me feel loathsome. So I loathe them for that in advance. Does that count as self-loathing?

A: Yes! And of a very creative kind, because you're not even sure that all of them do loathe you, and if they do, you aren't really sure why. In fact, you have to write all their lines for them out of your own head. Remember: the further your guess from reality, the more creative you are!

FIVE FROM SL4B'S PARANOIA SAMPLER

1. "They think I'm prejudiced just because I'm white."
Reality check: You happen to be both.

2. "Philip Glass is going to think I'm a musical moron for liking The Beach Boys."
Reality check: He's going to think you're a musical moron for assuming he's a music snob.

3. "She's not going to sleep with me because I'm not rich enough."
Reality check: She's not going to sleep with you because you'd rather assume what makes her tick than find out.

4. "They think they're better than me because I eat meat."
Reality check: True, but all that protein should give you enough strength to handle it.

5. "They hate us because we're free."
Reality check: Where to even begin?

SELF-LOATHING BY OMISSION

The easiest way to deal with social responsibilities is to focus on all the valuable things you are not doing, like voting, paying taxes, or thanking your mother-in-law for the book on female genital mutilation that she gave you as a wedding gift. That, and this worksheet:

I Am a Miserable Worm for Not . . .
(check as many choices as apply)

____ recycling my unused Greenpeace leaflets

____ jogging to stop a disfiguring and depressing disease

____ figuring out who my do-nothing representatives are

____ replacing all my incandescent bulbs with ugly, compact fluorescents

____ hiring a qualified applicant who was fat, old, lame, and depressed

____ protesting at least 50 of the world's 10,000,000 or more injustices

____ quitting: smoking, eating meat, driving

____ taking the trouble to understand any side but my own, correct one

____ caring about the Middle East

____ caring

Tip

Professional self-loathers, like ex-studio head Sherri Lansing, attempt to correct all their sins of omission one by one, in order to ascend to the status of "Great Human Being."

Warning: Beginners should attempt this only in hopes of becoming insufferable.

If you don't donate generously to help the poor, loathe yourself for being a Scrooge (a Leona Helmsley).

If you do give lavishly, loathe yourself for trying to buy salvation with cash (a Bill Gates).

CATAPULTING

As you may (but being inattentive, probably don't) recall, there's a type of "Who, ME?," or self-loathing denial where you expel your discomfort with yourself by hurling it at others. Nobody knows what provokes people to catapult (see "Does He or Doesn't He?" page 196), but it's a favorite of political self-loathers.

THREE CLASSIC "I SUCK, SO I'LL KILL YOU" MOVES

1. After losing a vainglorious war of conquest, denounce your nation's mortifying decadence and start a new, bigger, even stupider war. It worked for France after their Revolution, Germany after WWI and for the U.S. after Gulf War I!

2. Threaten to blow up anyone who accuses your religion of advocating violence. Some Muslim fundamentalists pulled this on Pope Benedict in 2007.

3. Too good a pacifist to express yourself through bloodshed? Shout out this battle cry to warmongers everywhere: "You are so full of hate, I hope you die!"

Q: Can I catapult my self-loathing back onto myself?

A: It sounds redundant, but yes, you can. In fact one of the all-time top variations of the Catapult is the Boomerang. To boomerang, simply catapult your personal self-loathing back onto a group that includes you, or closely resembles yours. If American, hate America or Americans; if Sunni, hate Shi'ites. If lower-middle-class, hate middle-class attitudes or lower-class values. If educated, hate middle-brows; if middle-brow, hate "intolerance," which includes more or less everyone.

THE ART OF CAMOUFLAGE

Q: What if other people's loathing of me is making me loathe myself for something I don't believe is wrong?

A: Move to San Francisco. That, or try . . .

THE HAGGARD METHOD

Ted Haggard, leader of the National Association of Evangelicals, devised this variation of the Rush Limbaugh or "oil on water" strategy (see Part I, Chapter 1, page 21) for boomeranging his self-loathing onto his own evil twin:

1. Choose a circle whose values feel toxic to you. (Ultraconservative churches that view your sexual preferences as abominable are ideal.)

2. Dress and speak like your adversaries—not for amusement or camouflage, but to experience the illusion of their acceptance.

3. Politically attack anyone who shares your "vices," and whose style you dislike (see Suitable Looks to Choose From, pages 71–73).

4. Get outted by your dealer and/or butt boy, or discovered texting a request to your underaged congressional page that he send you a photo of his penis (the Mark Foley substitution) or get busted for playing footsie with a vice cop in an airport men's room (the Larry Craig substitution).

5. As soon as the scandal has upped your self-loathing to fever pitch . . .

6. Repent, and receive the forgiving love you've longed for from the people who hate the real you.

7. Promise to change your spots.

8. Repeat cycle.

Roy Marcus Cohn (1927–1986), the late lawyer and political deal maker, has often been depicted in films and plays as an epitome of the self-loathing gay boomeranger, and a pioneer of unbending denial in the face of gale-force evidence. When a protégé of the overzealous communist-hunter Senator Joseph McCarthy, Cohn outed numerous gay men for "security" reasons, driving them from their jobs, even to suicide, while he himself consorted with male models. When confronted with the facts, Cohn would protest that he was too masculine to be a "fairy." To the bitter end, he insisted that it wasn't AIDS that was killing him. But it was. Verdict? Roy Cohn would have loathed Roy Cohn—had he ever made his acquaintance.

Warning: Never assume that all haters are self-haters. Many are self-worshippers who don't know any better.

TEST YOURSELF

Feeling too pleased with your ability to guess the answers to my questions? See if you can guess the questions that provoked the following answers.

ANSWERS TO 6 COMMON QUESTIONS ABOUT CATAPULTED SELF-LOATHING

(questions follow)

A1. Jewish girls for Nicole! What, are you kidding?

A2. Jews.

A3. Obama. Black can't pass for white; he *is* white.

A4. Join the Log Cabin Republicans or the cast of *The L Word.*

A5. Extremely successful Hollywood agents

A6. Suicide bombers who called in sick.

The Questions:

Q6. If I wanted to sleep with the most extreme social self-loather I could find, what group would I cruise first?

Q5. What is the only group that self-loathes more than successful Hollywood agents?

Q4. How can a lesbian express her self-loathing with greatest impact?

Q3. Who has an easier time passing for white, comedian Jack Black or presidential wannabe Barack Obama?

Q2. Who loathes themselves more: anti-gay Senator Larry Craig (see Haggard substitutions above) or philandering family-values preacher Jim Bakker?

Q1. Who's more self-loathing: Jews for Jesus or Jewish girls for Nicole Kidman?

ONE LAST QUESTION

Q: Now that I've gambled away my mortgage at an Indian-run casino, do I still have to loathe myself for having stolen their ancestral lands?

A: No; but you can loathe yourself for trying to buy a clear conscience like you'd buy a Navajo blanket.

Master of Social Self-Loathing: Art Spiegelman (1948–)

Widely credited with bringing the graphic novel into the literary fold, Spiegelman's Pulitzer Prize-winner, *Maus*, created a cultural niche in which the malaise of everyday self-loathers replaced the adventures of superheroes. He portrays himself as a guilt-ridden son of damaged Holocaust survivors, all of them mice in a world of Nazi cats. The teen heroine of *Ghost World*, Enid Coleslaw, whose name is an anagram of Daniel Clowes, her creator, was endowed by him with the "confusion, self-doubts and identity issues that I still have." And Cleveland file clerk, Harvey (*"American Splendor"*) Pekar, named his most recent graphic memoir, *The Quitter*.

THIS CHAPTER'S MANTRA

I felt sorry for myself
because I had no shoes,
even after I'd met
a man who had no feet.

PART IV
THE
SELF-LOATHING
ELITE

"I HAVE OFFENDED GOD AND
MANKIND BECAUSE MY
WORK DID NOT REACH THE
QUALITY IT SHOULD HAVE."

— LEONARDO DA VINCI,
DYING WORDS (MAY 2, 1519)

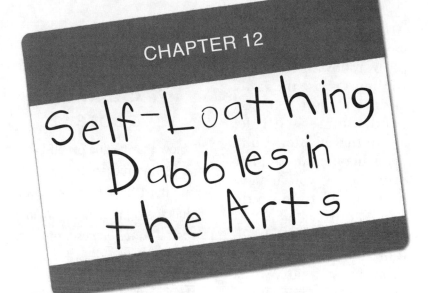

CHAPTER 12

Self-Loathing Dabbles in the Arts

"I'm ugly, shy, and anachronistic. But by dint of not wanting to be those things I have pretended to be just the opposite. Until today, when I have resolved to tell of my own free will just what I'm like, if only to ease my conscience."

—Nonagenarian narrator, *Memories of My Melancholy Whores* (2004), Gabriel José de la Concordia García Márquez

THE ARTS ARE a megastore of free information about what self-loathing can feel like and how it is best done.

Artists know, because you can't excel in the arts simply by following the rules; you must revise the rules, and you can't tell how good your revised rules are until well after you're dead. In other words, whatever success you achieve in your lifetime could prove entirely bogus.

BONUS AGONY-OF-CREATION QUOTE

"I know that feeling of self-loathing and feeling fucked up about the work. But I think that means you're doing the right thing."—*Johnny Depp to Darius James, author of* Negrophobia

I don't have to tell you that an open-ended trial by an invisible jury working without a fixed rulebook is the ideal opportunity for a self-loather like you to really get jiggy. Think about it: in the arts you get to self-loathe in four categories at once. You can . . .

. . . absorb disapproval from people who are afraid of change, including you!

. . . create impossible standards by which your work falls short.

. . . imagine circumstances that would leave your achievements in the dust—English replaced by txt msg! All analogue art quaint as tea cozies! Music custom-made inside people's heads with programmable implants!

. . . reflect upon all the stitches you've dropped while pursuing your obsession. Degrees! Relationships! Helping others! A life!

If you are feeling ambitious, you can also make your self-loathing the theme of your work, so that you have to wallow in your own muck, attuned to every smear and whiff of it. Get good enough at this, and loathing yourself in your chosen medium may be the only thing people will pay you to do, if they pay you at all.

FINE ART

THE MUSEUM OF THE VISUAL SELF-LOATHER: CLASSICAL PERIOD

Ancient Greek art, like today's fashion spread, is a pantheon of polished, well-toned Abercrombie & Fitch beings more attractive than you are. In Greek literature, men fall in love with marble statues instead of real women, much like men today fall in love with bodies made of silicone. In Greek mythology, women consort with gods who present themselves as bulls, swans, rays of light, anything other than short, hairy, jealous little Greeks. Greek art is still cherished today by conservative men as the taproot of self-loathing in Western Civilization.

RENAISSANCE GALLERY

Michelangelo di Lodovico Buonarroti Simoni (1475–1564), the great Florentine sculptor and muralist now known— like Cher—only by his first name, was a same-sexer who struggled with his church's anti-homosexual

Decoded

Leonardo da Vinci's famous *Vitruvian Man* (1492) revived the Greek notion of ideal human proportions. (Remember Self-Loathing Master Polykleitos, page 50.) Leonardo's version of Mr. Perfect makes arcs with his arms like a snow angel without snow, standing as if crucified against a circle in a square. Like us, he's a martyr to Euclidean ratios; because once physical perfection is precisely quantified, most of us can never measure up.

doctrine. Near the end of his life, after completing the Sistine Chapel ceiling and luxuriating in postpartum self-disgust, Michelangelo depicted himself on the wall behind the chapel's altar as an empty skin held up by a demon in Hell—a lesson to us all. And that lesson was? If you want a really fantastic ceiling, hire a gay guy who hates himself to paint it.

MODERN AND CONTEMPORARY ART

After the themes "I am a miserable sinner" and "We are all miserable sinners"—themes which, in addition to Bosch and Michelangelo, attracted the likes of Rembrandt, El Greco,

Saints Come and Go, but Our Demons Hang In There

The Dutch painter Jeroen van Aken, pka Hieronymus Bosch, went beyond expressing personal feelings of guilt to evoke twinges of self-disgust in the viewer. *The Garden of Earthly Delights* (ca. 1510) promises that everything our naked souls enjoy will be brutally destroyed in a fiery inferno by twisty little demons with frogs' legs, devilish grins, and Hannibal Lecter hearts. Centuries later, Bosch's jewel-like and terrifying images of damnation are still vivid evocations of the sort of self-loathing that makes Hell hell.

and Goya—the next big innovation in self-loathing art was Dada, in which artists declared art itself loathsome! Fresh from the trenches of WWI, where mechanized warfare turned sophisticated Europe into a slaughterhouse, the Dadaists pointed out that art's much-touted civilizing effects were nonexistent. At the height of the movement, Marcel Duchamp presented a "ready-made" urinal as a sculpture, implying (among many, many other things not relevant here) that artists were as much a bunch of piss-bags as everybody else—including you.

Art Assignment

1. Take two cocktail napkins.

2. On one, draw a picture of yourself as an empty skin.

3. On the other, depict all of human history as a cauldron of guilt and torment.

4. When you're done, wad them both up and throw them down a toilet, and you will have arrived at . . .

The Now

GALLERY NOTES

Match each of the artists in Column A with the statement in Column B that best suggests his or her self-loathing style:

A	B
1. Lucian Freud	A. I greatly enjoy defining my decadent historical moment.
2. George Grosz	
3. Francis Bacon	B. I loathe the horror of human existence, including my own.
4. Judy Chicago	
5. James Ensor	C. I loathe my face beneath this mask, and the damn mask, too!
6. Lisa Yuskavage	
7. Karen Finley	D. I loathe how everything pillowy and silly and soft about me betrays me when seen through the filter of gender stereotypes.
8. Trey Parker and Matt Stone	

Answers:

E. I loathe the chaotic visual information offered up by my body, or even Kate Moss's body.

F. I loathe my crazy, lurid, multicolored vagina; I'd rather it was a dinner plate.

G. I feel like I'm covered in caca, only art turns it into chocolate.

H. I greatly enjoy defining my decadent historical moment as poo.

1) E. Lucian Freud (1922–),

2) A. George Grosz (1893–1959) and F. Trey Parker (1969–) and Matt Stone (1971–)

3) B. Francis Bacon (1909–1992)

4) F. Judy Chicago (1939–)

5) C. James Ensor (1860–1949)

6) D. Lisa Yuskavage (1962–)

7) G. Karen Finley (1956–)

8) H. Trey Parker and Matt Stone

THE PERFORMING ARTS—THEATER, DANCE, AND MUSIC

THEATER

Although theater is where movie and TV stars seek refuge when they want to loathe themselves less, it is very big on self-loathing generally, particularly the kind that insists on hiding shameful secrets until Act Three. (In Act Three we realize that either the truth will make us free, or that life is sordid and meaningless and nothing will make us free, so why keep secrets?)

And here's the good news: theater is a great substitute for church! Just as handling snakes distracts you from the pain of being you, playwrights like Samuel Beckett, David Mamet, and Neil LaBute evoke a disgust with humanity that's every bit as entertaining as speaking in tongues.

YOUR QUESTIONS ANSWERED

Q: Who is the most inspiring self-loather in the history of theater?

A: That would have to be Hamlet, prince of Denmark. The setup is that the ghost of Hamlet's dad, the late king of Denmark, wants moody, sexy Hamlet Jr. to avenge his murder by killing the new king, Hamlet's uncle (and now stepdad). The prince doubts that the ghost can be trusted, but he spends the rest of the play loathing himself for not doing its bidding because, he thinks, maybe he's just a big pussy when it comes to spending eternity in Hell for regicide. While agonizing eloquently, he mistakenly kills an old fool; his neglected (possibly pregnant) girlfriend drowns herself in a stream (which everyone blames on him); and he kills his mother, the queen, by accident, too. The point is, Prince Hamlet packs a lifetime's worth of self-loathing into five acts, so that (spoiler alert) when he dies tragically in the end, you are nonetheless delighted that such a witty prince can suffer so much more self-doubt than you do.

For inspiring a self-loather with his Dark Family Secrets, Prince Hamlet is hard to beat. But he has stiff competition:

King of Dark Family Secrets

Several ancient Greek playwrights— including Sophocles and Aeschylus—wrote about King Oedipus of Thebes. As you know, the Oedipus myth is about an abandoned baby who grows up adopted and under a fateful curse, which he only learns *after* he has a) reached manhood, b) killed his father, king of Thebes, and c) answered a Sphinx's tricky riddle, thereby winning the hand of the queen, his mother. When he finds out that (unknowingly) he has committed patricide and incest, he so can't face himself that he puts out his eyes. Millennia later, Oedipus remains the Post-it boy for the self-loather's favorite maxim: "You don't have to *be* guilty to *feel* guilty."

Warning: Blinding yourself to express feelings of guilt is a memorable gesture, but it is not recommended.

Better to: (1) Announce to everyone, "Okay, that does it! I'm putting out my damned eyes!" (2) Chicken out. (3) Cry: "I'm not good at anything!"

DANCE

Q: Dance, ballet, modern, jazz—it's so uplifting and inspiring! Is it compatible with self-loathing at all?

A: Like athletics, dance asks people to deform their soft, earthbound bodies in order to achieve amazing things it is impossible for other bodies to do. Dancers' feats of power, grace, and expressiveness raise the bar for humanity, but they also raise the bar for you. Just thinking about ballet makes most people feel schlubbier and more sluglike when they shuffle out of their bedrooms in the morning or slide under the barstool at night.

MUSIC

Q: What's the best music to loathe myself by?

A: Music of all kinds makes a great accompaniment to any kind of self-loathing you want to do—romantic, physical, layered, catapulted, etc.

If you search creatively, you can find a song or symphony that will enhance them all. And your options are many. If you're sobbing your eyes out over how clueless you were about your lover running off and marrying someone his mother would like better than you, "Three Blind Mice" can highlight your humiliation as well as *Madame Butterfly*. Even a song like "Blue Skies" can sound like a dirge for happiness lost or missed. Anything in a minor key, anything about a breakup or a crime or hopeless longing, especially hopeless longing in the Middle East, and you should be off and running with a soundtrack that'll make your misery sing.

Q: What's the best song lyric for me to learn if I want to suffer from performance anxiety and achieve a high-level of professional self-loathing, like Johnny Depp?

A: You might try this from Millencolin's "Man or Mouse":

Yeah, yeah, yeah . . .
I hate myself when going
Yeah, yeah, yeah

See, there is no more piercing self-disgust than that of someone who wants to make an original contribution to his or her field, but is feeling mortifyingly derivative of the Beatles. Millencolin may not have broken out as a Top 10 act, but it has deftly conveyed how much self-loathing it can cost to try.

Q: Can self-loathing help my music career?

A: Possibly. (See the Inspiration Box, this page.)

Branded

Courtney Michelle Harrison, pka Courtney Love, actress and creator of the band Hole, was best known as the wife of Nirvana's Kurt Cobain, who famously said, "I'd rather be dead than cool." His suicide was a hard act to follow, but Courtney has managed to market her self-loathing as a brand, expressing it through spectacularly bad behavior. Thanks to her drug busts and public brawling, neither her legend nor her considerable talents were buried along with her more celebrated mate.

DEAD TREES

As you know from having read this far, world literature is a mother lode for self-loathers of every stripe.

Like Kafka (see Inspiration Box, this page), writers worldwide have used their own self-loathing and borrowed that of others to create countless tortured characters you can use as role models.

It's All Material!

The Czech absurdist Franz Kafka, although engaged twice (both times to Felice Bauer between 1912 and 1917), was too beset by sexual phobias to marry. What he did instead was to use the humiliating pre-engagement interview given him by his fiancée's parents as inspiration for *The Trial*, his great novel about free-floating guilt and arbitrary judgment.

YOU BE THE JUDGE— AND THE JURY

Decide which of the fictional characters paired below is most self-loathing, and defend your decision, as if anyone cares what you think.

Category: Self-loathing for not being able to close deals anymore

Defeated salesman Willy Loman in Arthur Miller's play, *Death of a Salesman*

OR

Defeated salesman Shelley Levene in David Mamet's play, *Glengarry Glen Ross?*

Category: Self-loathing for not being an aristocrat
Quixotic glamour addict Emma Bovary in Gustave Flaubert's novel, *Madame Bovary*
OR
Ambitious social climber Clyde Griffiths in *An American Tragedy* by Theodore Dreiser?

Category: Self-loathing for not having come from a sufficiently debased background
Middle-class fan of trailer trash, Earlene Pomerleau in Carolyn Chute's *The Beans of Egypt, Maine*
OR
Suttree, the middle-class man devolving into a river rat in Cormac McCarthy's novel by that name?

Category: Self-loathing by a Jewish man who fears his love for Gentiles won't be mutual
Alexander Portnoy, desperately seeking shiksas, in Philip Roth's *Portnoy's Complaint*
OR
Isaac Babel in *Red Cavalry*, "a man with spectacles on his nose and autumn in his heart," traveling incognito with a troop of manly, anti-Semitic, Cossack commies?

Category: Self-loathing for taking an unspeakable amount of crap from the white man
"I," the first person "new Negro" narrator in Ralph Ellison's *Invisible Man*
OR
Suicidal hausfrau Sylvia Plath in her book of poems, *Ariel?*

Category: Self-loathing for having been heartless and creepy and now doomed to suffer in a cruel and materialistic society in which your struggle to become a better person won't matter all that much

Floor-scrubbing ex-supermodel Veronica in Mary Gaitskill's *Veronica*

OR

David Lurie, white, sexist, washed-up Cape Town academic, in J. M. Coetzee's South African novel, *Disgrace?*

Category: Self-loathing for feeling guilty and not being sure why

K, on trial for crimes unspecified in Franz Kafka's *The Trial* (see page 172)

OR

The sin-soaked Underground Man in Dostoevsky's *Notes from the Underground?*

Category: Self-loathing for being a psychopath

Twisted ingrate, and pseudo-half-black adoptee Joe Christmas in William Faulkner's *Light in August*

OR

Lou ("all the time I'm laughing myself sick inside") Ford in Jim Thompson's *The Killer Inside Me?*

Category: Self-loathing because this too, too solid flesh won't melt

Tortured Hamlet in Shakespeare's play of that name (see pages 168–169)

OR

Hungry Esther Wells in Fay Weldon's novel, *The Fat Woman's Joke?*

If you give up on your artistic ambitions, you can feel bad for losing faith in yourself.

If you persist in the face of early failure, you can loathe yourself because you're unrealistic—doomed to disappointment and poverty.

JOIN A PALE MALE SYMPOSIUM*

* all quotations actual

Chuck Palahniuk: More and more, it feels like I'm doing a really bad impersonation of myself!

Stephen King: I am the literary equivalent of a Big Mac and fries!

Dashiell Hammett: I've been as bad an influence on American literature as anyone I can think of!

Elias Canetti (*sneers*): People love as self-recognition what they hate as an accusation.

Truman Capote (*nods*): When God hands you a gift, he also hands you a whip; and the whip is intended for self-flagellation solely.

John Dos Passos: Ha ha. If there is a special Hell for writers it would be in the forced contemplation of their own works.

Charles Bukowski (*drunkenly*): If you're looshing your shoal and you know it, then you've shtill got a shoal left to looshe.

You: I wrote a really bad _____ once.

Master Cultural Self-Loather: Simone de Beauvoir (1908–1986)

Author of the feminist classic, *The Second Sex*, de Beauvoir challenged the French intelligentsia's notion that "Woman" is a creature of nature rather than culture. Thanks to her success, women can now be ashamed of their failings as public intellectuals as well as their shortcomings as earth mothers. But she went further. As the short-stick-holder in a miserable "open marriage" with existentialist Jean-Paul Sartre, de Beauvoir demonstrated how a woman could be a strong, independent achiever while serving as a frog-like philosopher's doormat. Many newly empowered women have followed suit, from actress/activist Jane Fonda—whose "work it 'til it burns" exercise tapes funded her unfaithful husband's 1970s Senate bid—to, more recently, Hillary Clinton, who showed us how sticking by a powerful male philanderer can increase your self-loathing while setting you up for a presidential race.

ONE LAST QUESTION

Q: Do "creatives" so often loathe themselves because they see themselves clearly, or do creative endeavors just make you feel like dirt?

A: That question's too confusing. And not funny. Wording's awkward, stilted. Tone's uneven. It's a broken lamp. Fix it.

THIS CHAPTER'S MANTRA

Picasso had a
blue period; but
I am blue, period.

CHAPTER 13

The Spiritual Self-Loather

"Some men and women, indeed, there are who can live on smiles and the word 'yes' forever. But for others (indeed for most), this is too tepid and relaxed a moral climate. Passive happiness is slack and insipid, and soon grows mawkish and intolerable. Some austerity and wintry negativity, some roughness, danger, stringency and effort, some 'no! no!' must be mixed in, to produce the sense of an existence with character and texture and power."

—*The Varieties of Religious Experience* (1902), William James

MOST SPIRITUAL paths encourage one or more previously mentioned categories of self-loathing—from sexual to philosophical—in an effort to cure you of it. Faiths that attempt to purge a crowd of all self-hatred sometimes merely displace its fury. This can result in Inquisitions, fatwas, and hideous headgear. But most religions channel your desire to escape self-loathing into more benign rituals of atonement: a willingness to fast, for example, or to walk over hot coals for a mile on your knees. Alternatively, you can support your religious group by giving it money—the root of all evil. If the logic of these strategies escapes you, it is supposed to: that's why religious rites are called mysteries.

BONUS MEA CULPA QUOTE

"The good I would, I do not, and that I would not, that I do, O wretched man that I am." —St. Paul

WORLD RELIGION

FIND THE BEST SPIRITUAL PATH FOR PROCESSING YOUR TYPE OF SELF-LOATHING

To help you find a religion that's compatible with what you feel life is all about, here is a quick-and-dirty overview of major world belief systems.

Let Religions Process Your Self-Loathing

	Tribal Religions	Catholics	Protestants	Jews
Biggest Official Reason to Self-Loathe	Break taboo; fail to properly self-mutilate	Commit mortal sin	Fail to let Jesus into your heart	Break commandment
Worst Punishment for Above	Exile or shaming	Excommunication, damnation	Eternal hellfire	Payment to injured party
Way to Obtain Forgiveness	Spells, sacrifice	Confession, repentance	Let Jesus into heart	Donation to synagogue
Self-Loathing of This Type Reduced by . . .	More cows	Festival of guiltless drinking to honor saint	World domination	Nothing
Biggest Actual Cause of Self-Loathing	Mate isn't any good, and people pity you	Bad, bad urges	Having a body	Failure to excel
Best Way to Use Your Self-Loathing	Send kids to mission school	Pursue sainthood	Support imperialism	Write screenplay

Muslims	Buddhists	Hindus	Neo-Pagans	Atheists
Violate Koranic Law	Lack compassion	Violate Brahamaic law	Pollute Mother Earth	Lapses in skepticism exposed
Stoning, decapitation	Suffering	Return as computer virus	Earth destroyed	Invitation to publish rescinded
Not obtainable	Enlightenment	Make offering to gods	Give up meat, use CFLs, buy Prius	Submit evidence supporting evolution
Reading Barbara Cartland novels and expatriating	Audience with dalai lama	Election victory	Giving up old towels for organic cotton ones	Prayers answered; grants received
Western domination of your country	Poor meditation technique	Conflict with traditional mores	Gas-guzzling eco-vacations	Envy god-lovers who feel less despair
Persecute rival sect	Smile serenely	Create virus protection program	Light candle to protest global warming	Learn to live with it

> If you have faith, loathe yourself for being so gullible (sentimental, unquestioning).
> If you lack faith, wonder if you aren't too repulsively cynical (defeatist, a Grinch).

You may want to examine some religions in more depth before choosing one. So here is a short tour of the most popular.

THE WEST

Whereas Eastern religions tend to regard the self as a painful illusion that you should loathe yourself for believing in at all, Western religions openly encourage self-loathing as self-punishment for more specific sins.

THE JUDEO-CHRISTIAN BIBLE

The Bible is subject to as many interpretations as there are self-loathers. Theologians disagree on even the most basic questions, including: "Was the God of the Old Testament a self-loather or not?

Here are four of many opinions:

Opinion #1: Oh, he was a self-loather, and big-time.

After throwing the universe together in a manic rush and beholding its flaws (like the narrow birth canals of hyenas), the God of the Jews was so disgusted with Himself that He made His self-portrait—not out of gold like the other gods—but from mud and dust. He then animated it, named it "Adam," and blamed it (instead of His design) whenever it screwed up. Created as God's double and whipping boy, we are most like Him when punishing ourselves and those who remind us of ourselves.

Opinion #2: Yahweh only loathed Himself once.

It happened after He let Satan talk Him into torturing a devotee named Job, just to test Man's faith. Yahweh ruined Job's business, turned everyone against him, and covered him in painful boils, but Job refused to curse God—making Yahweh look more capricious and immoral than Eve! After giving Job back everything, Yahweh still felt guilty, so, in penance, He sent His only son to redeem "the meek"—those who still love Him when covered in painful boils. His self-revulsion thus soothed, Yahweh damned all of what He used to call His "chosen people" to eternal fire.

Opinion #3: No, no no! Why should He loathe Himself?

Yahweh, in His mercy, bestowed upon our weak and gullible species the gift of free will. So, when you err it's your fault, not His. Period.

Opinion #4: Oh, who knows?

Yahweh cannot be understood by lesser beings—like you.

EVANGELICAL CHRISTIANITY

Evangelical Christianity is the fastest-growing religion in the world, according to *Atlantic Magazine*. Join, and you are guaranteed eternal life (if you are willing to wait until you're dead to enjoy it), and also if you accept Jesus's love. Devotees choose different ways to interpret this bottom offer, however. Are there any here that suit you?

The Divine Love Worksheet

Jesus loves a wretched, miserable, abject sinner: *me!*

Jesus loves me, mostly because I'm not a Jew or a heathen or a feminist or a communist or homosexual, and because He is merciful.

Jesus loves me, but only provided I love Him a lot more than I love myself—which, ha ha, shouldn't be too hard.

Jesus loves me, but isn't attracted to me physically, so it's safe to kiss Him without looking gay (or nympho, or European).

Jesus loves me, so I guess it's okay that I'm such a loser.

Jesus loves me because I'm profoundly, totally, abjectly sorry for all the vile things I've thought and done and will do again soon—knowing me.

Jesus loves me, so I don't have to!

Jesus loves me, but may in His mercy send me to Hell forever if I don't love Him back.

BONUS CONVERSATION-WITH-SATAN QUOTE

"When I awoke last night, the Devil came and wanted to debate with me; he rebuked and reproached me, arguing that I was a sinner. To this I replied: Tell me something I don't already know!"—*Martin Luther*

SCIENTOLOGY

No one who is not one of Scientology's elect can be certain what it is that they believe in, but to outsiders it appears to be John Travolta and Tom Cruise.

THE EAST

ANCIENT EASTERN SECRETS OF SELF-LOATHING

Many today are abandoning the violently jealous Middle Eastern gods in favor of Asian spiritual disciplines whose music is softer and whose idols look better with designer furniture.

Here is a very rough guide to the showroom lines:

1. If you loathe yourself you are mired in false dualities, so smack yourself on the head with a cudgel. (Zen Buddhism)

2. The only way to end the torment of self-loathing is to stop believing the illusion of self altogether. This could take many, many, many, many, many lifetimes, some of them spent as a vole. (Hinduism)

3. Once you realize that self and world are both illusions, you enter the realm of pure consciousness and may meet Richard Gere. (Tibetan Buddhism)

4. Dude, the true nature of things is incomprehensible; and the cosmology bitches at Berkeley are on with it. Fuckin' hard core. Sick. (California Buddhism)

NEW AGE RITUALS FOR BEGINNING SELF-LOATHERS

New Age spiritual advisors treat self-loathing as a wound to be healed with ointments, legumes, biofeedback, and exercise. Ironically, it is the commercialization of New Age culture—crystals; turquoise; West Elm vases; tapes of running brooks; homeopathy; happy, woozy salespeople—that is most likely to inspire a self-loather to exchange the material world for another world—even a selfless one.

Here are a few of the actual recommendations you can find in Mike George's new age compendium, *1001 Ways to Relax,* along with *SL4B*'s suggestions on how to apply them to your self-abasing regime.

Relax————————————————Remember . . .

1001 Ways to Relax: "Imagine yourself as seaweed."
Your response: It'll be a step up for me.

1001 Ways to Relax: "Play to an empty theater."
Your response: With my talent, I'll have to.

1001 Ways to Relax: "Apply the same leniency to others as you do to yourself."
Your response: Look out everybody!

1001 Ways to Relax: "Meditate on a candle."
Your response: Ow!

1001 Ways to Relax: "See dying as a gift."
Your response: Oh, you shouldn't have!

YOUR QUESTIONS ANSWERED

Q: What about all the other one true religions and their sects, Quakerism, Baha'i, Zoroastrianism, Gnosticism, Mormonism, Christian Science, Sufism, Jehovah's Witnesses, Animism, Sunni Islam, Shi'ite Islam, Hassidism, the Zealots, the gurus, Unitarianism, and so on and on? Do any offer me a better way to create, control, and use my self-loathing? What about Satanism? Secular Humanism?

A: They're all equally good—provided that, like Mother Teresa, you maintain some tortured doubts.

Q: If my divine leader asks me to drink poisoned Kool Aid or leave my body behind so we can ride a spaceship to a better place, which course of action will make me loathe myself most?

A: Alas, both courses of action will rob you of your divine ability to suffer.

Q: If I truly believe, won't God's love wash all my self-loathing away?

A: Not unless you have exact change for God's washer.

Q: For a Catholic priest in good standing, is pederasty an abomination, or just something to pass the time between communions?

A: Well put.

WWMD (What Would Madonna Do?)

Raised Catholic, Madonna surfed to superstardom and disassembled her self-loathing by flaunting each of its forbidden components in a shameless way (see page 35). Now, in midlife, her strategy of self-loathing management can't work: looking your age just won't sell in the pop market. Unable to visibly age without shame, Madonna's creaky athleticism has become a kind of self-betrayal. So, like many other show-business adepts, she has entrusted her self-loathing to a religion. Interestingly, she snubbed Catholicism for Kabbalah, a once-feared esoteric branch of ancient Jewish mysticism that predates biblical laws. The version Madonna studies has been lightened up to attract a wider following. Having started her career as a bottle blonde with dark roots, the Material Girl, always stylish, has found a spiritual equivalent.

Q: How can I be sure that I'm experiencing self-loathing rather than demonic possession?

A: When your eyes light up, your head spins around, and your voice changes, it's usually demonic possession. That, or puberty.

Q: How can holy war increase my self-loathing?

A: Two ways—(1) start one (2) lose one.

Master of Spiritual Self-Loathing: St. Augustine (354–430)

The brilliant North African single father now known as St. Augustine spent his youth traveling, whoring, and teaching rhetoric. Then, in midlife, he rejected the two gods of the Manicheans—one evil, one good—for a purely good Christian god—who despised him. Seeking forgiveness for a youth spent barking up the wrong steeples, Augustine lovingly and vividly recorded his every vice and doubt in his *Confessions* (397–401). He has earned master status for showing generations of memoirists how to convert a lifetime of small personal regrets into durable literature.

ONE LAST QUESTION

Ex-Phish Groupie: Does being a Phish groupie count as a religion?

SL4B: You can't count any rock group as a god unless and until you are on your knees before them.

THIS CHAPTER'S MANTRA

God loves me,
especially when
I loathe myself.

CHAPTER 14

All in Your Mind

"I personally think we developed language because of our deep need to complain."

—Lily Tomlin

THE SELF-LOATHING mind is a fascinating, if elusive subject of study. Psychologists, neuroscientists, linguists, mystics, and philosophers have all taken pokes at it, and now, in a beginner-like way, so shall we.

We'll start by improving your self-loathing self-awareness. Next, we'll ask the basic questions about self-loathing that scientists and philosophers are wrestling with, like (as promised), "If there's such a thing as free will can I have some?" We'll wrap up by resolving a few centuries-old philosophical questions to prepare you for the next sections on death and graduation.

META-SELF-LOATHING

YOUR QUESTIONS ANSWERED

Q: When someone like Lily Tomlin, who does not believe in loathing yourself, loathes herself, and then loathes herself for loathing herself, what is it called?

A: If she blames it on her *Huckabees* director, it's called a meltdown, but if she keeps it to herself it's called meta-loathing. To get a mature and serene perspective on your self-loathing—like Tomlin's (when she isn't losing it)—start with this baby step:

1. Loathe something about yourself—for example, your knees.

2. Decide that loathing your knees is vulgar and vain.

3. Think, "Never mind that millions do it, I ought to be better than they are."

4. Ask yourself, "How come I am not?"

5. Conclude that it's because you're weak! And weakness is a loathsome character flaw.

See how you did that? You managed to loathe yourself for the way you loathe yourself! Even if you are a only a beginner, this paragraph should have given you some useful ideas—not only about how to grow disapproval of yourself in an organic and sustainable way, but also how to leaven the pain of it all with a childlike amazement at your inventiveness. With this new technique in your toolbox, let's proceed to the next step up.

Q: Is there any way I can structure my self-loathing so that it spirals higher and higher in a widening gyre without my having to work at it?

A: Yes; there's an advanced technique called *spiral self-loathing* in which you use each iota of self-loathing to connect to the next, pivoting around a central point but increasingly far from it, until the whole chain of association spins out and goes tornado on you. Here's how:

THE SPIRAL

Let's say you're in the mood to style your self-loathing into the shape of a tornado. And let's say some Very Famous Person asks you what you think of last week's sunny weather.

1. Be disgusted with yourself for not coming up with a fluid, witty riposte to the effect of, "Ah, the weather! It never rains, but it bores."

2. Hate yourself for caring too much about impressing the VFP.

3. Face it, being a groveling starfucker is your nature, and it's cruel of you to beat up on yourself for something you can't help.

4. Note that you are bullshitting yourself about your helplessness, and are (deplorably, self-indulgently) trying to let yourself get away with less than your best.

5. But so the fuck what? Hate yourself for taking all this shit too seriously.

6. A joke? Of course! The sunny weather question was meant as a joke! You should have come back with one about melting polar ice caps.

7. Next, think, Wait! The VFP was *already* joking about the ice caps and you missed it because of being so

slow, so cowed, so too-wrapped-up-in-your-insecurities to live in the moment!

8. If you are really adept at spiraling you can segue seamlessly from #7 into a critique of your current project or entire career, your abilities in general, your intimate relationships and so on.

In other words, spiral self-loathing is just like garden-variety self-loathing, only with all the connections tight and all the "I"s dotted.

Q: How does the human mind allow me to turn against myself in so many rich, rewarding ways?

A: One: Evolution. Your brain evolved from a long, elaborate buildup of animal wetware. Squid, chimps, and, eventually, Cleopatra, all have little programs installed on your system. The whole mess is loaded with bugs and legacy features carried over from life in the wild, and you can see in, for example, Elton ("Do you know who I *am?!?!*") John, that the relatively new processors in the prefrontal cortex sometimes develop conflicts with earlier ones.

Two: your nervous system runs on drugs; lots of drugs: serotonin and serotonin re-uptake inhibitors, adrenaline, cortisol, dopamine, oxytocin, estrogen, testosterone, even prions. And they like to party.

Q: So you're saying that the human mind, basically, is a sack full of zoo animals on drugs?

A: Basically, yes. And when the animals all pounce on each other you experience spiral self-loathing.

IS THE SELF AN ILLUSION?

Q: So if the brain is a system of assembled components, and the mind is a jungle preserve, complete with several eco-conscious nonprofit organizations that administer it, what is the "self"? Does it really exist, or is it just an emergent property of our compound nervous system, like the "mind"? And if the "self" encompasses all of me, including things like "mind," "identity," a sense of physical separation from other people, etc., what, exactly, does the loathing?

A: You do.

Q: But I'm an illusion.

A: Yes, but your self-loathing isn't.

FREE WILL

Q: You're telling me that feuding sections of my brain meet in committee and make decisions, and that's how I get free will?

A: Well, science isn't sure about that yet. Because numerous parts of the brain run themselves behind your back. When Hugh Grant, shortly after breaking up with Jemima Khan, started kicking a persistent paparazzi, it's possible that adrenaline had bypassed his thought processors and went straight to the "kill the paparazzi" part of his brain, causing him to "go off" uncontrollably. Numerous studies reported by Malcolm Gladwell in his book, *Blink*, explain that your brain starts doing most, if not all, the things you do before you "decide" to do them or even know that you are about to. That is, your hand has often started to insert coins in the vending machine before your mind has decided to cheat on your diet.

Q: So, between genetics and our circuitry, we don't always have free will?

A: Well, and add culture. A lot of European philosophers say that your culture does most of your thinking for you—your language, the power structure you live under, the ideas you inherit from other generations—those things determine what you can and can't "choose" to think.

Q: Doesn't having so little control over who I am make me pathetic?

A: If you choose to think that.

Q: So then, whether or not to loathe yourself after doing something stupid is the only free choice I have?

A: I wish I could confirm that, but self-loathing is often preconscious, too. You can begin experiencing it long before you have mentally linked that sinking, imploding feeling to your having just won an 18th-century porcelain figurine in an online auction when you know that the rent is due in a week and you owe back taxes and you're a sucker with the self-control of a toddler.

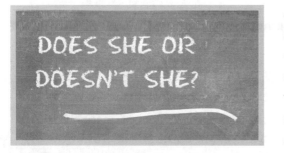

After being sentenced to community service for throwing a mobile phone at housekeeper Ana Scolavino's head, supermodel Naomi Campbell apologized: "I felt very remorseful for having thrown the phone at someone that didn't deserve it," she told ExtraTV. "I have a deep sense of shame for the things I've done." She expressed her shame by wearing designer clothes on her way to her penance job at the sanitation department, followed by a number of high-profile interviews, showcasing her new sense of responsibility. Throwing the phone may not have been an act of free will, but exploiting her self-loathing was. Verdict: A real pro.

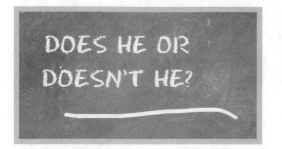

Did Mel Gibson tell his arresting officer that "Jews caused all the wars in the world" because he is misinformed, because he feels that if he doesn't please his bigoted father he's worthless, or because he was trying to beat himself up and the Jews just happened to get in the way? Verdict: Only Jesus knows, because Mel doesn't. His self-loathing is unconscious, and he likes it that way: curled up, catnapping on the radiator of his mind, waiting for someone to open a can of tuna—or a bottle of tequila.

Q: Are you saying that, basically, morality comes from your gut?

A: Ask Joshua Greene and Jonathan Cohen. The two Ivy League neuroethicists study how the mind makes moral judgments. They've concluded that the "common sense" moral framework people use is usually inappropriate and can even lead to disaster. You not only get to sin before you know it and loathe your sins before you know it, but you also get to loathe yourself for not knowing for sure what they are!

BONUS YOU-ARE-SO-CLUELESS QUOTE

"In personal and in public life . . . whenever one has the agreeable sensation of being impressively moral, one probably is not."

—*George F. Kennan in "Morality and Foreign Policy,"* Foreign Affairs, *Winter 1985–6 issue*

ANCIENT PHILOSOPHY AND SELF-LOATHING

Self-loathing and classical philosophy have a lot in common. Both question people's relationships to themselves, both make your head hurt, both require you to think of all possible objections to what you just said, and both bore the pants off your friends and your dry cleaner.

FOUR ANCIENT QUESTIONS

Ancient Question #1: If I could erase half my self-loathing, then half of what remains, then half of that, and so on infinitely, would it take me an eternity to eliminate it all?

Ancient Answer: Try it and see.

Ancient Question #2: Seriously, if I loathe everyone everywhere, myself included, am I a self-loather or a misanthrope?

Ancient Answer: "Or"?!? It's "and." You should have that one down by now.

Ancient Question #3: Descartes said, "I think, therefore I am." As a self-loather can I say, "I think, therefore I suck?"

Ancient Answer: No; as a Cartesian self-loather you have to say, "I am, therefore I suck." Descartes thought that thinking makes you suck less.

Ancient Question #4: What's more fundamental—to loathe myself for what I am or for what I do?

Ancient Answer: Am? Do? Self-loathing precedes both existence and essence, Being and Nothingness. All evidence suggests that it was formed at the very moment when matter parted company with antimatter and duality was born. Some theorists make the extravagant claim that self-loathing (along with anger, anxiety, and wishing you had a bigger house) is a combination of both dark matter and dark energy, comprising as much as 96% of the mass and energy in the universe.

The point is: you can loathe yourself for what you are, for what you do, AND for a lot of reasons you haven't managed to come up with yet, but will. And when it gets to be too much, you can escape to the sunny 4% of the universe where tiny, subatomic particles of self-love abound.

 ## Master of Humanity's Self-Loathing: The Simpsons (1989–)

In answer to the ancient question, "What is the nature of humankind?" Matt Groening's animated series *The Simpsons* proposes that we are a procession of bumblers beguiled by selfishness and vanity, tripped up by sentimental attachment to unworthy objects, and frequently slapped by self-rebuke, or as Homer says: "D'oh!" In other words, dignity is not, for our species, a ride we're tall enough to get on. But we make our creator laugh.

ONE LAST QUESTION

Q: If a tree falls in the forest, and nobody hears it, will I still loathe myself?

A: Yes! Because your philosophy books waste so much paper that soon there will be no trees left. And it'll all be your fault.

THIS CHAPTER'S MANTRA

A mind is a terrible thing to, um . . . have?

CHAPTER 15

Endgame

"It's not whether you get knocked down. It's whether you get up again."

—attributed to Vince Lombardi

OPPONENTS of self-loathing will encourage you to view death as a natural transition, but you'll get more out of it if you see it instead as a shameful failure to stay alive. Only the rankest amateurs among us refuse to accept responsibility for things we can't control.

OLD AGE

Even if you have been a closet self-loather all your life, on your deathbed, you are expected to make a big show of self-denunciation. This is the time to (1) repent of your flaws and misdeeds, (2) pray for absolution from your deity, and (3) beg forgiveness from those you've cut out of your will.

But why wait? You can start blaming yourself now.

The aging process offers a thousand ways to rev up your self-loathing in anticipation of that final day. Many older self-loathers, seeing their hopes die and their beauty crumble like a moth kept too long in a jar, try to blame time; but to blame time for your damage is a kind of buck-passing.

Besides, self-castigation has a fortunate side effect: it will make you die sooner than those who blame their shortcomings on others (or so nursing home statistics suggest). Since blaming yourself for every mishap will shorten your suffering and the misery of everyone around you, you are selfish if you don't do it.

DECLINE

Mercifully, long before you cut to the final chase, you may have decades in which to savor your slow decline from (1) desirable cupcake to (2) battle-scarred beast to (3) terrifying grotesque. You may choose to humor those chipper cheerleaders who assure you that you "look good," or have "a young spirit," but it's a good idea to join up with others to protect your right to detest old age and to be appalled with yourself as you suffer through its heinous indignities. Here is a membership card that admits you to ARSH, The Association for Retired Self-Haters.

THIS IS TO CERTIFY THAT _____

IS A MEMBER IN GOOD STANDING OF THE ASSOCIATION OF

RETIRED SELF-HATERS.

The ARSH pledge: We hold these truths to be more or less true, that any-one over the age of 50 has an inalienable right to make frequent jokes about disintegration of body and mind, repulsive and humiliating medical procedures, past regrets, sexual dysfunction and the existential horror of mortality without fear of attitude correction by others, no matter how cer-tain those others might be that a more positive attitude towards yourself will make you feel better. This is not to say that you shouldn't get a break on medical insurance, early suppers, and movie tickets.

Signed, Adam Haversham, President, ARSH

NORA EPHRON—HATES HER NECK AND HER PURSE: WHAT CAN YOU HATE AS YOU GET OLDER?

(Now that you have a license to complain, take your time filling in the blanks.)

The way my _____ looks in jeans.

The fading tattoo on my _____.

That my _____ hangs down when I bend over a lover.

The wrinkles on my _____ that make me look like the an elephant's _____.

That my mind can no longer retrieve my children's _____s or _____s.

That when hairs now grow out of my _____ instead of my ____ I can't see them without glasses.

The pain in my ____ and my ____ and my _____.

The prospect of having my _____ and my _____ replaced.

The way my _____ swells and my _____ does not.

INVESTMENT OPPORTUNITIES

Thanks to the prankishness of modern medicine, average life expectancy is now in the high 70s, so that increasing numbers of old people will lack:

—Adequate protection against quacks, con persons, and identity thieves

—Adequate protection against elder abuse

—Adequate Social Security

—Adequate medical insurance

—Adequate savings

—Bladder control

First, avoid putting all your chips on Depends™, because when the boomer generation turns 70, the majority won't be able to afford them, and landfills will be too full of adult diapers to hold more.

Invest in scams that claim to eliminate elder self-loathing, because that's where demand will swell. Tea that makes urine smell like gardenias is a good place to start.

FALL

Not every old codger will be sitting in puddles of gardenia-scented urine while ordering inspirational videos off the Internet. Thanks to the worldwide growth in income disparity, the well-off will have jewel-encrusted urine pads; and their ample self-loathing will be jewel-encrusted, too.

The way old wealthy people usually express their hatred of themselves for aging is to "fight it," which means that they will end their lives looking like Joan Rivers: embalmed, but lively. But there's nevertheless an awkward age for rich and powerful oldsters—the 20 to 40 years between their last big triumph and their obit in *The New York Times*. In that interval, many can only escape late-life regrets by either getting sailed around in a yacht with a personal masseur or going soft in the head.

The upshot is that even octogenarian billionaires will have to depend upon Jamaicans and Colombians to loathe them when they are no longer able to loathe themselves.

DEATH

YOUR ONLINE QUESTIONS ANSWERED

boobytubular840: As my life winds down, how can I avoid the serenity and self-acceptance that occasionally strikes people in their dotage?

SL4B: Try telling your children that you plan to leave everything to Anna Nicole Smith's daughter.

Doyenne

Fashion mogul Donatella Versace is currently the Old Elvis of haute couture. In 2007 she told *The New Yorker's* Lauren Collins, "People have a low perception of me, men especially. They think, 'This woman, she's a nightmare.'" But Donatella's efforts to hide her age (that "My Little Pony" mane, those Mickey Rourke collagen lips) are beyond hideous. Ever since the murder of her brother Gianni in 1997, her continuous awareness of death has turned her into one of those Tibetan demons whose terrifying image you hang on the wall in hopes of keeping worse monsters at bay.

MMisMMMGOOD: Isn't an early and spectacular death like Marilyn Monroe's the most dramatic and stylish way to express self-loathing?

SL4B: For telegraphing self-loathing, most experts agree that early and spectacular death pales beside sleeping with two Kennedys.

MMisMMMGOOD (again): If I can't sleep with two Kennedys, how can I make my death a testament to self-loathing?

SL4B: On your deathbed, try to come up with embarrassingly self-effacing and undignified last words, like, "Here goes nothing," "Last words, blah, blah," or "Th-th-th-th-that's all, fuh-fuh-folks."

DOTARD-IN-A-TUTU: If I haven't accomplished anything worth remembering, how can I leave behind a legacy of self-loathing after I'm gone?

SL4B: Choose one of these three self-deprecatory epitaphs:

1. "Here lies . . . oh, who cares?"

2. "Go ahead, walk all over me."

3. "Finally!!"

ONE LAST QUESTION

Q: Can I stop loathing myself after I die?

A: Probably not.

Masters of Endgame Self-Loathers: Robert Chester Wilson Ettinger (1918–) and Aubrey de Grey (1963–)

Robert Chester Wilson Ettinger and Aubrey de Grey developed and popularized the concept of cryonics, in which your body is frozen solid, to be thawed at some later time once a cure for whatever you died of (including freezing) has been discovered. Biogerontologist de Grey is working to expedite scientific methods of rejuvenation, hoping that within this century, his cellular and molecular interventions will allow people to become immortal. Thanks to these two, and others like them, you may soon be able to loathe yourself eternally!

THIS CHAPTER'S MANTRA

I don't deserve to die.
Or, no, wait:
Maybe I do.

APPENDIX

". . . I NOW ASKED MY
COMPANION WHICH WAS
MY ETERNAL LOT? HE
SAID, BETWEEN THE
BLACK & WHITE SPI-
DERS. . . ."

—WILLIAM BLAKE,
"THE MARRIAGE OF
HEAVEN AND HELL"
(1790-1793)

Graduation

LOATHING LESSONS LEARNED

If you have read this book through, memorized your mantras, and completed all the quizzes, you can qualify as an advanced self-loather upon completing and flunking yourself on the following.

OPEN-BOOK EXAM

1. *True or False*

a. The only thing worse than the pain of self-loathing is what happens when you try to get rid of it. T__ F__

b. Self-loathing isn't everything; it's just one more thing I'm not perfect at. T___ F___

c. Self-loathers tend to produce less than non-self-loathers, which, given the worthless crap most people produce, is a good thing. But, oh shit: I'm ranting again; sorry. I hate curmudgeons. Like me. T___ F___

d. People who have never experienced self-loathing are simply not paying attention. T___ F___

2. Which five of the following are not known types of self-loathing?

Utter, Partial, Part-time, Paranoid, Parental, Parfait-style, *Fried egg,* oil-slicked, *coal-fired,* catapulting, changeling, Time-release (aka "Old Elvis"), *Kate Moss,* Lite, *Subcutaneous,* Unconscious, *Mistaken?*

3. Defend your answer to the following in under 20 words. All answers are correct, so you will be judged on charm, grace, originality, form, wit, elegance of expression, and (where appropriate) balls. What is the best all-purpose tool for a self-loather?

a. a three-way mirror

b. the Holy Bible

c. a blind date

d. a factory-farmed pork chop

e. a highly evolved brain

f. the universe

g. my organs of "replication."

4. What is the Seventh Essential Element of self-loathing after: (1) a clear sense of self, (2) a belief system (however transient), (3) a willingness to violate your beliefs, (4) a self-critical streak, (5) a talent for seeing though your best self-deceptions, and (6) an ability to feel disgusted?

5. If you can only afford food or medication, which should you buy, and why is it all your fault that you are forced to choose?

6. If you could have more than one self to loathe, how many would you seek for this purpose, and why?

7. Compose your own self-loathing mantra based on this opening:

Poems are made by fools like me, but _____

Pending completion of this test, and your willingness to assign yourself a grade lower than you are capable of earning, you may fill out your diploma, to be found on the following page.

Further information about self-loathing, along with a T-shirt you can buy and more are available at www. sl4b.com.

Self-Loathing School

Diploma

This certifies that

_____

has completed a b.s. (beginner's stratum) course
in introductory self-loathing and is acquainted
with the basics, the essentials, and a variety of
the more common options for increasing, directing,
balancing, and styling self-loathing. The bearer
is qualified to practice advanced self-loathing
without a license anywhere that self-loathing
licenses are not legally required.

This document does not qualify the bearer to teach self-loathing or to
hire out as a motivational speaker at self-loathing seminars without
written permission from the author.

Witnessed this _____ day of ____, 20__

Signed _____*Lynn Phillips*_____

Acknowledgments

THANKS TO all those who made self-loathing—the book and the experience—a pleasure to get through. Nick Ellison, my agent, has cleared hurdle after hurdle for this project and never faltered. Santa Monica Press has been a responsive and creative collaborator (and funny). Thanks also to Scot Crawford, David Kaplan, Ellen Scott, Kurt Opprecht, Jeanne Johnson, Michael Singer, and Ruth Kreitzman for helping me to bag the metaphorical garbage and leave it on the curb, and to Kathy Maloney and Jim Raglione for keeping me moving and breathing so that I wouldn't overdose on this topic. Also to Justine Rendall, a great friend much missed, who died trying to keep her chin up.

Author's Bio

LYNN PHILLIPS is a media tramp who writes and edits for film, television, print, and interactive media.

She was a staff writer for the groundbreaking satirical nighttime soap opera, *Mary Hartman, Mary Hartman.* After working as a scriptwriter for several major studios, she moved back East where she has written for a wide array of publications from *Glamour* and *The Realist* to *The Harvard Lampoon.*

Under the name "Maggie Cutler," she wrote "The Secret Life of Kitty Lyons," a bimonthly column for *Nerve* (www.nerve.com), the Web and print magazine. Still pseudonymous, she wrote for *The Nation*; co-created the satirical political websites, www.vaguepolitix.com and www.shacklereport.com; and was a regular contributor to *Newsweek International*'s "Letter From America."

She and her husband live in New York with one cat—a self-loathing adept—who, having licked the fur off her thighs, has taken the pseudonym, "Poodle."

BOOKS AVAILABLE FROM SANTA MONICA PRESS

WWW.SANTAMONICAPRESS.COM • 1-800-784-9553

The 99th Monkey
A Spiritual Journalist's Misad-
ventures with Gurus, Messiahs,
Sex, Psychedelics, and Other Con-
sciousness-Raising Experiments
by Eliezer Sobel
312 pages $16.95

The Bad Driver's Handbook
Hundreds of Simple Maneuvers
to Frustrate, Annoy, and Endan-
ger Those Around You
by Zack Arnstein and
Larry Arnstein
192 pages $12.95

Calculated Risk
The Extraordinary Life of
Jimmy Doolittle
by Jonna Doolittle Hoppes
360 pages $24.95

Captured!
Inside the World of Celebrity Trials
by Mona Shafer Edwards
176 pages $24.95

Creepy Crawls
A Horror Fiend's Travel Guide
by Leon Marcelo
384 pages $16.95

Dinner with a Cannibal
The Complete History of
Mankind's Oldest Taboo
by Carole A. Travis-Henikoff
336 pages $24.95

Educating the Net Generation
How to Engage Students in the
21st Century
by Bob Pletka, Ed.D.
192 pages $16.95

The Encyclopedia of
Sixties Cool
A Celebration of the Grooviest
People, Events, and Artifacts of
the 1960s
by Chris Strodder
336 pages $24.95

Exotic Travel Destinations
for Families
by Jennifer M. Nichols and
Bill Nichols
360 pages $16.95

Footsteps in the Fog
Alfred Hitchcock's San Francisco
by Jeff Kraft and
Aaron Leventhal
240 pages $24.95

French for Le Snob
Adding Panache to Your
Everyday Conversations
by Yvette Reche
400 pages $16.95

Haunted Hikes
Spine-Tingling Tales and Trails
from North America's National
Parks
by Andrea Lankford
376 pages $16.95

How to Speak Shakespeare
by Cal Pritner and
Louis Colaianni
144 pages $16.95

James Dean Died Here
The Locations of America's
Pop Culture Landmarks
by Chris Epting
312 pages $16.95

L.A. Noir
The City as Character
by Alain Silver and
James Ursini
176 pages $19.95

Led Zeppelin Crashed Here
The Rock and Roll Landmarks
of North America
by Chris Epting
336 pages $16.95

Movie Star Homes
by Judy Artunian and
Mike Oldham
312 pages $16.95

Redneck Haiku
Double-Wide Edition
by Mary K. Witte
240 pages $11.95

Route 66 Adventure
Handbook
by Drew Knowles
312 pages $16.95

The Ruby Slippers,
Madonna's Bra, and Ein-
stein's Brain
The Locations of America's
Pop Culture Artifacts
by Chris Epting
312 pages $16.95

Rudolph, Frosty, and Captain
Kangaroo
The Musical Life of Hecky Kras-
now—Producer of the World's
Most Beloved Children's Songs
by Judy Gail Krasnow
424 pages $24.95

School Sense
How to Help Your Child Succeed
in Elementary School
by Tiffani Chin, Ph.D.
408 pages $16.95

Self-Loathing for Beginners
by Lynn Phillips
216 pages $12.95

Silent Traces
Discovering Early Hollywood
Through the Films of Charlie
Chaplin
by John Bengtson
304 pages $24.95

The Sixties
Photographs by Robert Altman
192 pages $39.95

Tiki Road Trip
A Guide to Tiki Culture in North
America
2nd Edition
by James Teitelbaum
360 pages $16.95

Tower Stories
An Oral History of 9/11
by Damon DiMarco
528 pages $27.95

The Ultimate Counterterrorist
Home Companion
Six Incapacitating Holds Involv-
ing a Spatula and Other Ways to
Protect Your Family
by Zack Arnstein and
Larry Arnstein
168 pages $12.95

ORDER FORM 1-800-784-9553

	Quantity	Amount

The 99th Monkey ($16.95

The Bad Driver's Handbook ($12.95)

Calculated Risk ($24.95)

Captured! ($24.95)

Creepy Crawls ($16.95)

Dinner with a Cannibal ($24.95)

Educating the Net Generation ($16.95)

The Encyclopedia of Sixties Cool ($24.95)

Exotic Travel Destinations for Families ($16.95)

Footsteps in the Fog ($24.95)

French for Le Snob ($16.95)

Haunted Hikes ($16.95)

How to Speak Shakespeare ($16.95)

James Dean Died Here ($16.95)

L.A. Noir ($19.95)

Led Zeppelin Crashed Here ($16.95)

Movie Star Homes ($16.95)

Redneck Haiku ($11.95)

Route 66 Adventure Handbook ($16.95)

The Ruby Slippers, Madonna's Bra, and Einstein's Brain ($16.95)

Rudolph, Frosty, and Captain Kangaroo ($24.95)

School Sense ($16.95)

Self-Loathing for Beginners ($12.95)

Silent Traces ($24.95)

The Sixties ($39.95)

Tiki Road Trip ($16.95)

Tower Stories ($27.95)

The Ultimate Counterterrorist Home Companion ($12.95)

		Subtotal	_____
Shipping & Handling:		CA residents add 8.25% sales tax	_____
1 book	$4.00	Shipping and Handling (see left)	_____
Each additional book is	$1.00	**TOTAL**	_____

Name _____

Address _____

City _____ State _____ Zip _____

❏ Visa ❏ MasterCard   Card No.: _____

Exp. Date _____ Signature _____

❏ Enclosed is my check or money order payable to:

Santa Monica Press LLC
P.O. Box 1076
Santa Monica, CA 90406

www.santamonicapress.com   1-800-784-9553